Jaisalmer
Life and Culture of the Indian Desert

Jaisalmer

Life and Culture of the Indian Desert

Photo
Oki MORIHIRO

Text
M.A. KONISHI
Kodai KONISHI

DK PRINTWORLD
Publishers of Indian Traditions

Cataloging in Publication Data — DK
[Courtesy: D.K. Agencies (P) Ltd. <docinfo@dkagencies.com>]

Morihiro, Oki, 1929-
Jaisalmer : life and culture of the Indian desert / photographs, Oki Morihiro ; text, M.A. Konishi, Kodai Konishi.

p. cm.
Includes bibliographical references (p.).
ISBN 13: 9788124606599

1. Jaisalmer (India) — Social life and customs — Pictorial works. I. Konishi, Masatoshi, 1938- II. Konishi, Kodai, 1975- III. Title.

DDC 915.44 23

First published in India, 2013

ISBN 13: 978-81-246-0659-9

Printed and published by:
D.K. Printworld (P) Ltd.
Regd. office: *'Vedasri'*, F-395, Sudarshan Park
(Metro Station: Ramesh Nagar), New Delhi – 110 015
Phones: (011) 2545 3975, 2546 6019; *Fax*: (011) 2546 5926
e-mail: indology@dkprintworld.com
Web: www.dkprintworld.com

Contents

Acknowledgements

The following figures in the text have been taken from the original sources listed below. Our thanks are due to those authors and publishers.

Figs. 1.1, 1.3, 1.4, 1.6 & 1.7: Kulbhushan and Minakshi Jain, *Mud Architecture of the Indian Desert*, Ahmedabad: AADI Centre, 1992.

Fig. 1.2: John D. Smith, *The Epic of Pabuji – A Study, Transcription and Translation*, Cambridge: Cambridge University Press, 1991.

Fig. 1.5: Kamiya Takeo, "Jaisalmer in the Thar Desert", *AT — Special Issue in Jaisalmer* (http://www.kamitjp/04_jaisall.html).

Fig. 1.8: L.N. Khatri, *Jaisalmer: Folklore History and Architecture*, Jaisalmer: Morchang Publication.

1

History and Culture of Jaisalmer
The "Golden City" in the Desert

M.A. Konishi

"**Jaisal Fort** . . . stands majestically poised on the hilltop overlooking the city on its slopes, glistening with a golden hue as it greets the first rays of the rising sun. It changes its mood at midnoon and looks like a sparkling sword of a Rājpūt warrior in the midst of a battlefield. At sunset the hot, dust-laden winds blowing from the desert sands impart yet another tone of beauty resembling that of a rugged worker . . . coming back home after a day's hard-toil. In the cold nights with starlit sky, the city, with blinking lights, looks like a lone ship anchored in a forlorn harbour in the vast stretch of desert-sand. On a moonlit night, the palaces, *havelīs* and tall buildings appear shining against the backdrop of the sandy desert." [Agrawala 1979: 79]

An Overview of Jaisalmer

Either coming by the dusty long-distance bus or by a train from Jodhpur, 290 km away through the arid and rugged desert lands of the Thār, one would at last see a vast stretch of the fortified city of Jaisalmer in distance, floating like a huge flat *jahāẓ* (ship) on the endless ocean of sand. Being situated in the midst of the vast desert of west Rajasthan, it looks like a mirage or a scene of *déjà vu* dream at the first sight, but it's real. The whole city shines golden with yellow sandstone used for the buildings against the background of the yellowish colour of the desert, turning to burning red during the sunrise and at sunset. At a closer look intricate stoneworks covering each and every surface of the buildings with the decorated balconies or bay windows (*jharokhā*), trellis (*jālī*) or the bower called *chatrī* in a typical style produce the delicate but sharp arabesque patterns of light and shadow under the strong sunbeams of the day [*fig.* 1.1].

This is the historic capital city of the Bhāṭī Rājpūts since the mid-twelfth century CE, with a history full of heroic events and deeds of the *rājā*s and the romance of princes and princesses. In spite of the harsh geographical settings, the city served as an important trading centre for a very long time on the extended caravan routes through the huge desert connecting the adjacent regions both in Gujarat and Sindh. It has also served as a safe refuge and shelter for the *rājā*s in ceaseless conflicts and for the rich adventurous merchants. When surrounded by the vast desert around them, the Fort rose like an isolated island in an endless ocean. However, the sporadic oases available in and around Jaisalmer could safely guard the society within the desert, and at the same time, it could help extend trade

1: Latticed window of a decorated balcony called *jharokhā* at *dīvān* or prime minister, Nāthmal-kī-Havelī. Notable is the intricate lace design so minutely interwoven from the skilful stone carvings. (previous page)

and communication contacts with other worlds far from here, through the far-reaching land-routes and networks of communication established by men and trade. The city flourished since the twelfth through the eighteenth century when the notable buildings of palaces, temples and *havelī* mansions were built in the city under the patronage of the rich *rājā* and some leading merchants.

However, the city lost its flourishing glory when the choice shifted to sea faring trade after the mid-nineteenth century through the Arabian Sea and the Indian Ocean without having to cross the tedious inland desert of Thār. Even more, the historical trading land-route became defunct by the creation of international border between India and Pakistan from 1947. The city has no doubt again acquired an important new strategic position as the westernmost district headquarters of the Republic State of Rajasthan in India, quite near to the border of Pakistan — only 70 km from the town. We all remember the recent nuclear test carried out in the desert of Pokharan; it was also in this border area to the east of Jaisalmer. It reminds us of the irony that even a historical and cultural heritage site like Jaisalmer town cannot remain dormant and peaceful in this shrewd and scheming contemporary world.

Rajasthan or Rājpūtānā, the Land of the Rājpūts

Rajasthan state extends on both sides of the Aravalli Range of the North-western part of the Indian Subcontinent. The North-western side of the Range is Mārwāṛ, that is more or less identical to the former domain of the Jodhpur *rājā*, and the other side is Mewāṛ that was the domain of the *rājā* of Udaipur. Both regions differ from each other in dialect, customs and manners, etc. due to the historical circumstances and geographical positioning, especially the difference in climate [*fig.* 1.2].

In Mārwāṛ, to which Jaisalmer belongs, the climate is dry and hot if compared with Mewāṛ where the climate is milder than the former. Most part of Mārwāṛ is just desert, forming the larger part of the Thār, or the Great Indian Desert extending from the south-eastern part of the lower Indus basin of Pakistan. The rainfall is generally very meagre and unreliable, and at present averages only 150 mm a year, and there is no perennial river running in the district except for a few *bāḍī* (dry river-bed) such as Lūnī (salt river) and some sporadic small saline lakes called *dhand*.

fig. 1.1: Jaisalmer Fort perched on the Trikūṭa Hill [Jain & Jain 1994].

2: Jaisalmer Fort glowing like a huge diamond at the sunset. A particular spot called "Sunset Point" is a big attraction for the tourists. The Fort shining like gold in the first rays of the rising sun is equally beautiful, giving the city its name the "Golden City". Foundation of this capital city was laid in the later half of the twelfth century on an isolated hillock in the desert, called Trikūṭa, 75 m high from the ground level. The present Fort is dated from the fifteenth century to the later half of the sixteenth century, and is the second oldest in Rajasthan; the first being Chittorgarh.

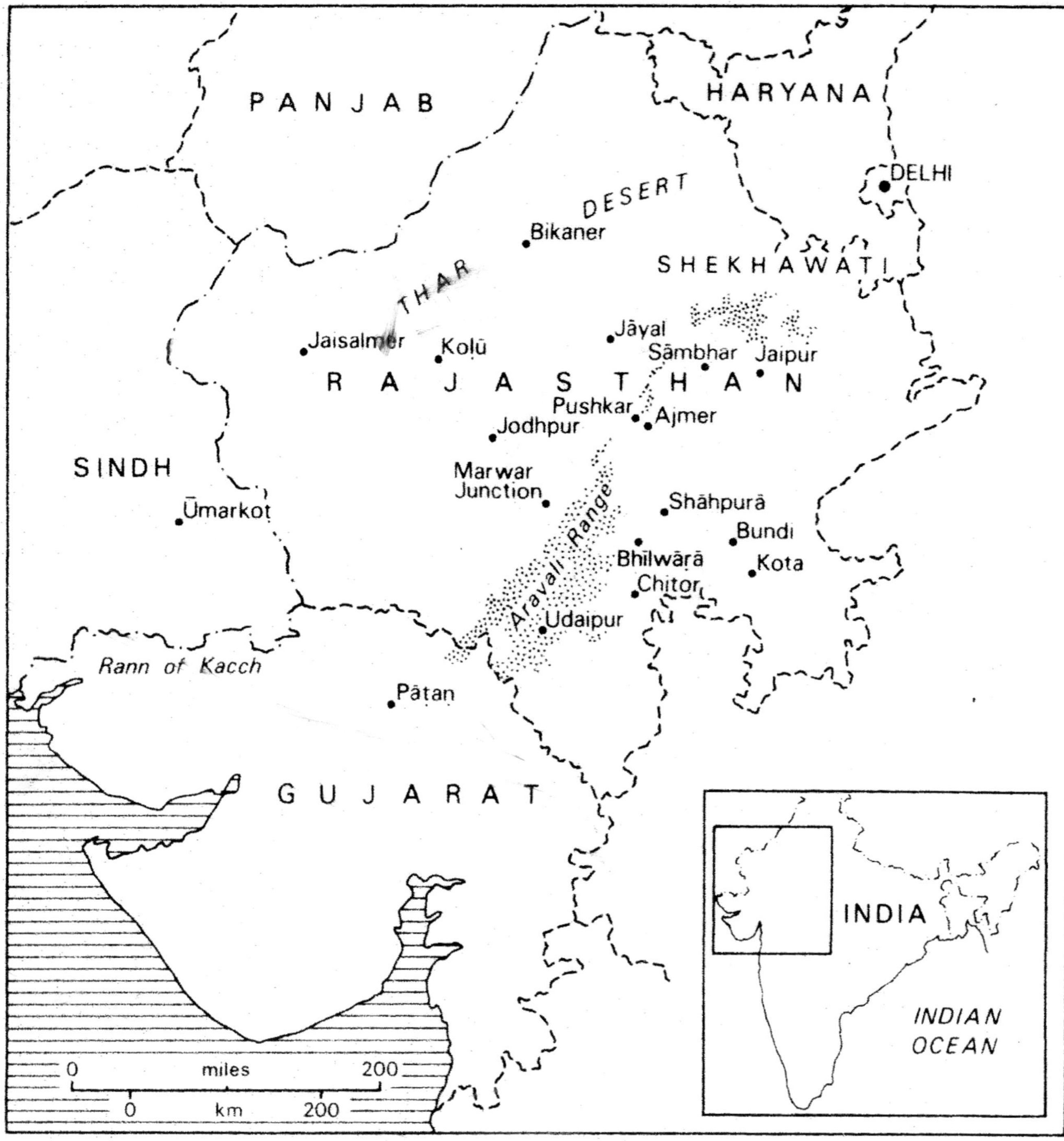

fig. 1.2: Map of the State of Rajasthan [Smith 1991].

The main source of water for the city has been Garisar Lake just beyond the outer fortification of Jaisalmer on its southern side.

At some places where the impervious clay beneath the sand still holds up groundwater, people would excavate wells in such places; but in ancient time, a branch of the present Sutlej River as an extension of the legendary and now dried up "Lost Sarasvatī" could have been running across the land from north to south almost parallel to the present course of the Indus, running right by the side of its eastern bank. Recent satellite photos have detected some prehistoric sites belonging to the third to the first millennium BCE, and archaeological explorations and excavations also have revealed pre- to mature Haṛappan (Indus Valley) Civilization and later chalcolithic sites, especially around Bikaner or nearer to Kutch in Gujarat including such important urban Haṛappan centres like Kālībaṅgan and Dholāvīrā. However, we still do not have ample evidence of the prehistoric sites in and around Jaisalmer itself, in spite of its great archaeological potentiality.

Historically, Rajasthan is the ancient Rājpūtānā or the "Land of Descendants of *Rājā*s and the great warriors". They have been collectively called "Rājpūts" or the "Sons of the Rājā (*rājaputra*)", but the origin of the Rājpūts is rather obscure. According to their own traditions, the Rājpūts are claimed to be the descendants of the ancient Kṣatriya *varṇa* (caste) belonging to the Solar and Lunar dynasties. Their brave deeds are sung in the ancient epics, but without any epigraphical evidences to support it till the first half of the seventh century, when they appeared as a warrior class. By that time, they might have already been mixed up with the alien populations from the West including the Gurjaras who entered India along with the Hūṇas in fifth century CE. They were even in close connection then and later with the indigenous tribes like the Gond, Kol, Bhīl or Bhar holding strong arms to form their own kingdoms and states. Rājpūts were, therefore, originally an occupational group of warriors rather than a consistent *varṇa* descendants — being composed of diverse people later lumped together as "Rājpūts" during the mediaeval time.

They became prominent in various areas in the North after the eighth century, by forming the dynasties like Pratīhāra in Kannauj (eighth-eleventh century), Cauhān or Cāhamāna in Rajasthan (tenth-twelfth century), Chandella in Central India (tenth-thirteenth

3: Massive rampart of the Fort in three layers with the long corridor and small rooms within. The oldest part of rampart was constructed in CE 1155, and was reinforced by a series of renovations five times. The main part was constructed in the fifteenth century during the reign of Mahārāval Lakṣmī Singh, that was further reinforced with the 2nd and 3rd ramparts during the sixteenth century by the succeeding rulers. The last reinforcement was carried out during the eighteenth-nineteenth century. (next page)

4: Round stones are still seen resting on the edge of the wall. They were once used as a sling during the closer battles. (next page)

4

5: Eastern corner of the rampart as seen from the Royal Palace. Massive ramparts constructed in three layers in the fifteenth-sixteenth century are clearly visible from the top of the hill, and the vast extension of the lower city can be seen beyond the Fort, along with some of the ninety-nine semi-circular bastions, also constructed in double layers along the fort wall.

century), Paramāra and Cāḷukya-Solaṅkī in the West (tenth-thirteenth century), Gāhaḍavāla in the North (eleventh-twelfth century), etc. The period from the eighth to twelfth century was thus the golden time of the Rājpūts but it was also the time when the Muslims started penetrating into India repeatedly from the west, and the Rājpūts had to fight long and strenuous battles against them. But they were too independent-minded respectively even within their own clan, and as such had no concern to unite themselves as one against the alien forces. They were rather always busy with their own internal conflicts and feuds. They still had been always brave and heroic, chivalrous and patriotic worth being sung in the local epics, but in due course of time, they also had to come under the sovereignty of the Islamic Delhi Sultanate in the thirteenth century and subsequently of the Mughals in the sixteenth century, although with short but heroic setbacks from time to time. It was during these troublesome periods when the Bhāṭī Rājpūts, a branch of the ancient Yadu Rājpūts, marked the beginning of history of Jaisalmer in the western-most part of Rajasthan.

Geographical Setting of Jaisalmer

The present district of Jaisalmer is bounded by Bikaner (India) and Bahāwalpur (Pakistan) on the north, by Khairpur in Sindh (Pakistan) on the west, by Barmer and Jodhpur on the south, and by Jodhpur and Bikaner districts on the east. Continuity of environmental and cultural characteristics with the adjoining districts in Pakistan particularly in the north and west is therefore quite obvious. Jaisalmer is, in fact, the largest district in Rajasthan (38,401 km^2) but it holds a very thin population (672,008 in 2011), the density being only 17 people per square km. However, the population has been slightly increasing over the last 10 years, as the population density was only 9 persons per square km in the 1991 census!

Most of the land in Jaisalmer district is a desert or a "wasteland". And the enormous amounts of the sand from the Thār covering the land surface can be seen typically in the vicinity of the villages of Khūrī, Sam and Rāmgaṛh around Jaisalmer. Geologically, the sand projects from the Vindhyan Jurassic and the Tertiary inliers, themselves largely sandstones, and the sporadic solid rocky hills represent the Lower Gondwana Talchir Boulder Bed. Rocky hills of granite and rhyolites around Jaisalmer extrude from the Aravalli surface, and along with the limestone mines in Rāmgaṛh or Amar Sāgar and yellow marble quarry at Habur, they all have formed the rich sources for the architectural materials to construct the beautiful buildings of Jaisalmer city throughout the history [Sharma, N.D.].

Landscape surrounding the city may look rather barren and monotonous but the sand dunes called *ṭībe*, varying in size from 3 to 15 km across, show beautiful wavy patterns on their slopes, changing their shape hour by hour due to the blowing winds. Colour of the sand dunes also changes from pale yellow-ochre to shining red or gold according to the time of the day, or season of the year [Agrawala, 1979]. This desert is not actually a "lifeless" monotonous world but, in fact, full of life and colours, though generally concealed from our eyes beneath the accumulated sands. Gay and colourful attires particularly of the ladies are in sharp contrast to the otherwise seemingly monochromic scenery of the desert. Chivalry of the Rājpūts and their rich cultural traditions of art and architecture, or oral epics sung with music and dance in typical Jaisalmerī style, are the products of this land, nurtured by the harsh natural environment.

There are no perennial rivers or water sources in the region except for a few lakes called *sar* such as Garisar and Amar Sagar, or the sporadic salt-marshes along the dry *bāḍī* or riverbeds. Rainfall is quite sparse, only 150-170 mm a year on an average, but when it rains, it may suddenly bring about a fresh life fed by water of the *bāḍī*, changing the orchards instantly green with colourful flowers. However, the climate remains generally harsh and dry otherwise.

Temperature in the mid-summer at the daytime in May-June may go up even up to 50° C, and in a cold winter night in December-January, it falls down below the freezing point. They, the locals, could not therefore rely on agriculture in such a setting, growing millet like *bājrā* or *jowār* only, but mostly depending on pastoral economy, grazing cows, camels, goats and sheep. Rich and ambitious people in the city, especially the Oswāl Jains, have been energetically engaged in trading and money-lending business and other services, including the tourist business in more recent years. Furthermore, oil deposits came to be discovered recently in a nearby place, and as the Indira Gandhi Canal Project is bringing abundant water since 1987, development in agriculture is also expected to be on the rise.

6: Lower city as viewed from the Royal Palace within the Fort. From here rulers could at once command a sweeping view of the whole city spread in crowded clusters. (next page)

7: An old-fashioned iron cannon set at a vintage point on a bastion of the outer wall. There are as many as ninety-nine bastions along the rampart to guard the Fort. (next page)

6.

7

8

9

Population of the city was around 35,000 in the high-time when Jaisalmer was the centre of the inland trading routes, but it came down to 4,000 at the end of the nineteenth century. It was due to the change of the trading routes from the land to the maritime, as also due to the political troubles and economic exploitation during the colonial rule of the British. But after the Independence in 1947, the population again steadily rose to around 20,000 in 1981, and was roughly 58,300 in 2001, more than 11 per cent of the total population of the district.

Inhabitants of the city are largely Bhāṭī Rājpūts, but there are also the rich Oswāl Jains, Hindu Brāhmaṇs, and Muslims including the converted ones, who all live in harmony. They hold on to their own traditional way of living but identify themselves as "Jaisalmerī". The land and climate have been so hard for the life of the inhabitants here, but other occupational *jāti*s together with the "tribal" groups like Jāṭ, Sonī, Jogī, Bhīl, etc. have also enriched the area, in spite of the harsh socio-natural environment.

Historical Background of Jaisalmer

Besides the legendary ancestry of the Yadu/Yādava Rājpūts in the lunar lineage tracing back their origin to Kṛṣṇa of the *Mahābhārata* in early centuries, the name of Bhāṭī was born by as early as the fifth king in CE 623 and had been used since then as their clan name. They had been moving around Punjab and the Thār being pushed by the approaching Muslim invaders, but became prominent in the tenth century when Bhāṭī Devarāja, ruler of Devagaṛh (present Derāwar), eleventh of the genealogy, attacked and seized present Loḍarvā (*c.* 16 km north-west of Jaisalmer), occupied then by the Loḍrā (or Roḍrā) Rājpūts. Since then the new rulers assumed the title of *rāval*/*mahārāval* instead of *mahārājā* to start their royal genealogy.

Loḍarvā was a typical fort on a hill (*giri-durga* or *prāntara-durga* as classified in classical texts), but was not secure enough. The Fort was soon attacked by Maḥmūd Ghaznī in 1024/25 on his way to seize Somnāth in Gujarat, and also by Muhammad Ghorī in 1103 and 1152.

*Rāval*s, however, regained the power in the twelfth century even under the reign of the Ghorī. According to Jain [1972: 369-72], the town was still in the possession of Bhojdeva in 1163, but his uncle Jaisala, 17th of the genealogy, conspired against him and seized the town. However, the town had been much deserted due to the

8: A series of *jharokhā*s or the decorated balconies projecting out from the Royal Palace. It is the most typical scene to showcase the glory of the marvellous architectural heritage of the city. (previous page)

9: The Fort as seen from the "Sunset Point", with the Royal Palace to the right. The Fort wears many different hues according to the time of the day and the seasons. (previous page)

fig. 1.3: The expansive Jaisalmer Fort at south-west corner of the City [Jain & Jain 1994].

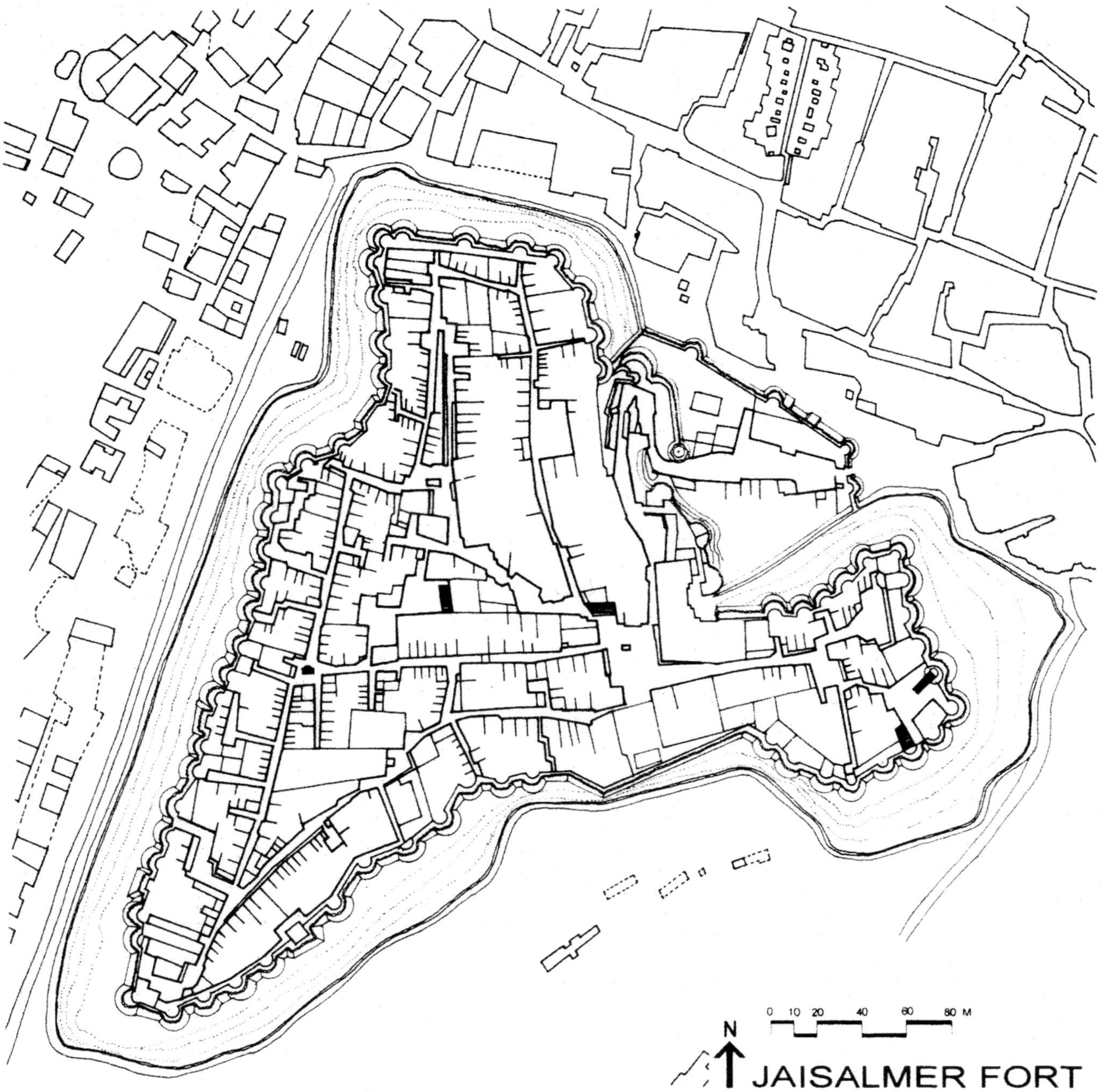

10

11

12

13

repeated attacks by the Ghorī, so he shifted his capital to Jaisalmer (then called Jaisalgaṛh) some time after that.

Therefore, chronologically speaking, it should be only after this event in mid-1160s when the foundation of the fort and the city was laid in Jaisalmer, and not in 1155 or 1156 (Vikrama Saṁvat 1212) as is generally believed, simply following Todd [1829: II-268] and others' records. Loḍarvā could still have remained as an ancient centre of the Jain culture for a while even after it lost the political/economical power, but the new place, Jaisalmer, was obviously safer to defend and wider enough to be the new capital to flourish with active trade and commercial activity [*fig.* 1.3].

The reason why the first *mahārājā* or Mahārāval, Jaisala, selected this place as his capital was totally strategic. It is situated on a higher hill and is surrounded by the vast expanse of desert all around (viz. *dhanvana-durga* or *dhanū-durga* in ancient typology). It also proved as well to be the best place for the east-west trading centre across the desert, and we can even now see the flourishing merchants' activities that are evident from their old magnificent *havelī*s (mansions) in the city. Presence of sweet water as in Garisar Lake on the foothill, and the rich hunting area surrounding the site must have also attracted the rulers to settle down here.

Several *rājā*s followed Jaisala, and Jaitasiṁha (r. 1276-99) among them was the most powerful ruler of the Bhāṭī dynasty ruling over Jaisalmer. But he and his successors had also to face the repeated attacks by Allā-ud-Dīn-Khiljī of Delhi (r. 1296-1316) and other Muslim principalities as well as the neighbouring Rājpūt forces like the Rāṭhods in Jodhpur, who had extended their power at a time even over Jālor and Ajmer. Their heroic bravery in the battlefields and the chastity of their wives, who committed *johar* immolating themselves at the death of their husbands is so well known and sung by bards in poems and epics, or played in string-puppet shows (*kaṭhputlī*) and painting narrations (*paḍ-vāčño*) by the Bhopās even to this day.

After Jaitasiṁha, nearly 20 other rulers (almost all the names are well recorded) succeeded the genealogy for another three centuries or so, enjoying prosperity and establishing the typical Jaisalmerī culture [Jain 1972: 372-74]. While other Rājpūt rulers had been engaged in internal conflicts, Jaisalmer remained relatively peaceful, so as to attract rich merchants and bankers from various

10: The interior of the topmost *mahal*, viz. Raṅgmahal of the Royal Palace. These mural paintings by *fresco secco* or of tempera technique could be belonging to the third quarter of the nineteenth century done under the influence of Jaipurī style, but yet with a later and local accent. This particular style goes on for about a century more, and is adopted in certain *havelī* murals, too. (previous page)

11: A wall painting of the Royal Palace depicting a battle scene. Here the colonial touch to the painting is evident, including the uniformed battalions and the newer expressions of the blue sky and floating clouds in the horizon. (previous page)

12: Śrīnāthjī or an incarnation of Kṛṣṇa holding up Govardhana hill, painted on the wall of the Palace. This type of painting, called *pichwāī*, drawn on cloth is a famous product in the sacred town of Nāthdvārā near Udaipur, Mewar. Mahārāvals or the Mahārājās of Jaisalmer have been devout Vaiṣṇavites in faith. (previous page)

13: Lord Śiva, Pārvatī and Gaṇeśa resting in peace on Kailāsa Mountain. Other than these religious wall paintings, Hindu themes in sculptures are quite limited, in spite of the rich tradition of stone carvings as is apparent from rather secular figures like *nāyikā*s or *apsarases* seen in abundance in Jain temples. (previous page)

other places to add further prosperity to the city to evolve it beyond the status of a refugee zone. In fact, from the beginning of the sixteenth century to the end of the eighteenth century, Jaisalmer witnessed a great progress and advancement in business, as well as art and culture. It was a safe place for all religions and castes, and the city became an international centre for trade, especially of cereals, *ghee* and opium. The trade extended even up to Afghanistan and Sindh, Iraq and Iran.

Among the great rulers of Jaisalmer, the name of Lūṇakarṇa is particularly worth remembering, as he had opposed even the Mughal emperor Humāyūn (1508-56) in 1541 while on his way to Ajmer via Jaisalmer. However, Jaisalmer seems to have been placed later in a somewhat subordinate position under the Mughals, though not as a mere subject state of the Empire. The *rāval*s had tried to keep matrimonial relationships with the Muslim royalty also, and the rulers of Bikaner and Jaisalmer (Har-rāj, 1560-77) gave their daughters in marriage to Emperor Akbar (1542-1605) in 1570. A chief of Jaisalmer also gave his daughter in marriage to a Turkoman Governor under the Arghun dynasty, and the son from this marriage was Khān-i Zamān, a highly distinguished general of Sindh of the time. During the time of Jahāngīr (1569-1627), Rāval Bhīma or Bhīm Singh's daughter was married to the Emperor and was listed as one of the 500 *manṣabdār*s or a fief-holder under the Mughals, and his brother Kalyāṇ Dās was appointed Governor of Orissa in 1610, and made a commander of 2000 soldiers six years later. Emperor Shāhjahān (1592-1666) rewarded Sabala Siṁha with the legitimate distinction as the ruler of Jaisalmer by the merit of his having saved the Mughal treasures from the Afghans in Peshawar.

This was really the political high time of the state, as it annexed the districts of Bahāwalpur, Jodhpur, Bikaner, etc. and served as one of the most active trading centres of the time. But from the time of the accession of Mūlarāja II (1762-1820), the fortunes of Jaisalmer rapidly declined, and its boundaries began to shrink. On 12 December 1818, the ruler had to conclude a security pact with the British East India Company to be recognized for the royal succession. Moreover, Salīm Singh, *dīvān* or the prime minister of Mūlarāja II and the next *rāval* Gaj Singh (1820-46) severely oppressed the Pāliwal Brāhmaṇs who had so far supported the economic and cultural wealth of Jaisalmer. The latter were forced to leave and evacuated the villages that were to be soon deserted.

14: Daśahrā (Dussehra) festival celebrations to commemorate the victory of Rāma over the Evil. The event is celebrated annually in the Palace courtyard, with the Mahārājā on the top of the stairs. The king is divine as the Rāma personified, thus the yearly renewal of kingship is surrounded by the aura of theocracy. (next page)

15

16

17

18

Colonial rule by the British had begun to get established in various parts of India by then, and Jaisalmer also finally went under the British paramountcy after 1818 at the time of Mūlarāja II. Land-route trade now gave the way to the trade across the sea, and the port cities on the seafront in Gujarat, etc. came to be more prominent. The new railway networks connected the inland cities as well, and the caravan cities of the old days lost their importance and glamour.

Further, the Partition/Independence of India and Pakistan in 1947 further cut the trade route between the Sindh and Rajasthan running through Jaisalmer because of the hostile state border.

The rich merchants and traders of Jaisalmer then left the city one by one leaving behind the vacant mansions or *havelī*s and moved to big cities like Bombay (Mumbai) and Calcutta (Kolkata) where they came to be known under the general name of *Mārwāṛī*. The city with a massive fort and many gorgeous *havelī*s were thus neglected to decay rapidly, and some parts of them, if not the royal palaces, looked like a ghost town, until the fort and buildings went through the careful conservation, preservation and restoration measures taken by the Federal and the State governments only a few decades ago to meet the archaeological and tourist interests.

Town Planning of the Fortified City

The South Asia has a long history of town planning since the Indus Valley Civilization, and Sanskrit texts like the *Vāstuśāstra* and the *Mānasāra* give detailed plans and manuals about how to plan a city. The ancient idea is beautifully reflected in the fortified city of Śiśupālgaṛh in Orissa dating back to 200 BCE and even for the city planning of Jaipur in Rajasthan, planned in CE 1728. However, no definite town planning as a whole, like the above, can be observed in Jaisalmer, where it seems that the city developed more or less in an organic way in and around the fort, like the other old cities in West Asia. Still, this is not simply a chance agglomeration of built-up forms, but somewhat of a planned growth. Observing keenly, the clusters of houses are built along the lanes separating the blocks more or less regularly, or, lining along the straight streets, where the houses are with a narrow entrance. But they are actually quite deep inside, often with a courtyard in the middle, and are packed on both sides of the streets. It is interesting to note that the entrance of each house does not face each other beyond the street, thus helping keep a sort of privacy.

15: Daśahrā procession inside the Fort to commemorate the victorious return of Rāma from Laṅkā after defeating Rāvaṇa. The Mahārājā, or Mahārāval as he is called here in Jaisalmer, is identified with Rāma, the ideal divine ruler of the country. (previous page)

16: Mahārāval Brij Rāj Singh-jī, the Mahārājā of Jaisalmer, leading the procession with a retinue of palace officials and valets. (previous page)

17: Mahārājā entering the Palace in dignity for the ceremony, led by a minister. The beautifully carved balcony and trellis walls of the Palace are noteworthy. (previous page)

18: Mahārājā sitting on the throne under a big silver canopy, receiving gifts and tokens as a sign of royalty from the retainers dressed in colourful turbans, and bestowing the boon in return promising a happy and prosperous rule. (previous page)

The sense of unity felt in this unique city is due also to the decorated façades and balconies, as well as the projecting windows from the houses and the spacious courtyards inside. The essential plan, even with the upper storeys with stairs but only without the balconies, follows the traditional aspects of ancient houses since protohistoric time in this arid part of the subcontinent, as we see in the ancient city of Moheṅjo-Dāṛo and others. Seemingly, lack of the total town planning of Jaisalmer should be rather due to the limitation of flat space on the top of the high hill, 75 m above the surrounding ground, where the fort was constructed essentially for security reasons. Even after the lower city was formed on the slope of the hill, buildings were constructed in two or three storeys, very close to each other. If the buildings could not extend horizontally, they had to be extended vertically thus competing in height upwards.

The first and the foremost intention of selecting this place as the new capital for the founder Jaisala was essentially strategic in nature to guard against the attacks, and the massive hill of Trikūṭa was quite appropriate to construct the fort. Classical texts classify several types of forts, and some of them like *giri-durga* (hill-fort or fortress), *prāntara-durga* (citadel on a hill), or *dhanvana-durga* (citadel in the desert) would fit the case of Jaisalmer [Kane 1973]. *Manusmṛti* (VII.71) and other Dharmaśāstra texts tell us that *giri-durga* stands best for the defence purposes, but the desert surrounding the fort would have also served the same purpose, as well as facilitating the trade-routes to remain open to the other regions, bringing in wealth to the city if it was properly guarded by the massive high ramparts (*parighā-durga*) as in Jaisalmer.

Historically, *giri-durga* or the citadel on a hill, would have been the oldest type in Rajasthan seen since the eighth to the thirteenth century. Loḍarvā belonged to this category having the palace and temples on top of the hill, but the flat space on the top was too much limited, so the capital was shifted to the present site of Jaisalmer some 16 km away. During the fourteenth and the seventeenth century, especially after the mid-sixteenth century, a fortified city came to be formed at various places in Rajasthan. Citadel was built on top of the hill with fort-palaces, garrisons, temples and gardens, but the space was still limited. That is why at Jaisalmer the fortified Lower Palace or City Palace had to be built on the slope of the hill, and the lower city for the citizens was laid further below. All these structures were however surrounded by the long and massive city wall or *parkoṭā* to form an entity as an integral fort-city. Agricultural lands, reservoirs and wells, or cemetery were all placed outside the city gates (*pol*), but the gate itself and its vicinity was the most colourful centre for the gathering of merchants and citizens, particularly on the occasions of the weekly *bāẓār* (*hāṭ*).

Similarly, the Jaisalmer Fort was first built as *giri-durga* or the citadel on a hill of Loḍarvā in mid-1160s, only with a *pol*, with some walls, temples and palaces at the first stage. But during 1577 and 1623, especially during the reign of Bhīm Singh, Sūraj Pol facing east was constructed, and Gaṇeśa Pol and Hawā Pol were opened soon. Furthermore, three-layered massive ramparts with 99 *burj*s (bastions) at a regular distance were constructed towards the end of the sixteenth century or the beginning of the next century [Tillotson 1987: 122]. Most of the bastions (92 out of 99) were meant for setting up the cannons, and the stone cannon-balls are still seen resting on the bastion walls [*Pl.* 1.4].

The lower city of Jaisalmer was formed after the construction of the fort to meet the demand of the growing population [*fig.* 1.4]. It was in *c.* 1722 during the time of Akhai Singh that the city started extending towards east, and the city wall surrounding the whole city was constructed in 1750 at the time of Mūlarāja I; so all the buildings of the lower city are to belong to the eighteenth century and later. The city wall had four main gateways, and two of them, Garisar Pol and Amar Sāgar Pol, were important as they were to connect the city with the water sources.

Crowded houses and narrow lanes give an impression of a typical congested city of the East, but we are also impressed by the sense of harmony and the order of the city by the horizontal lines marked by the balconies and terraces, and the standardized height of the building units. The orderly sense is further accelerated by the thorough use of yellow sandstones, that shine from yellow to red and thus give the whole city a strong impression as the "Golden City"; but it is equally striking that there seems to have been no city-planner or strong administrative intervention for the entire city planning. Jain [Jain & Jain 1994: 8] puts that it could be the result of the spirit of the people who sought for an environment which responded to the forces of nature like climate and sandstorms.

fig. 1.4: Whole layout of Jaisalmer City and Royal Complex [Jain & Jain 1994].

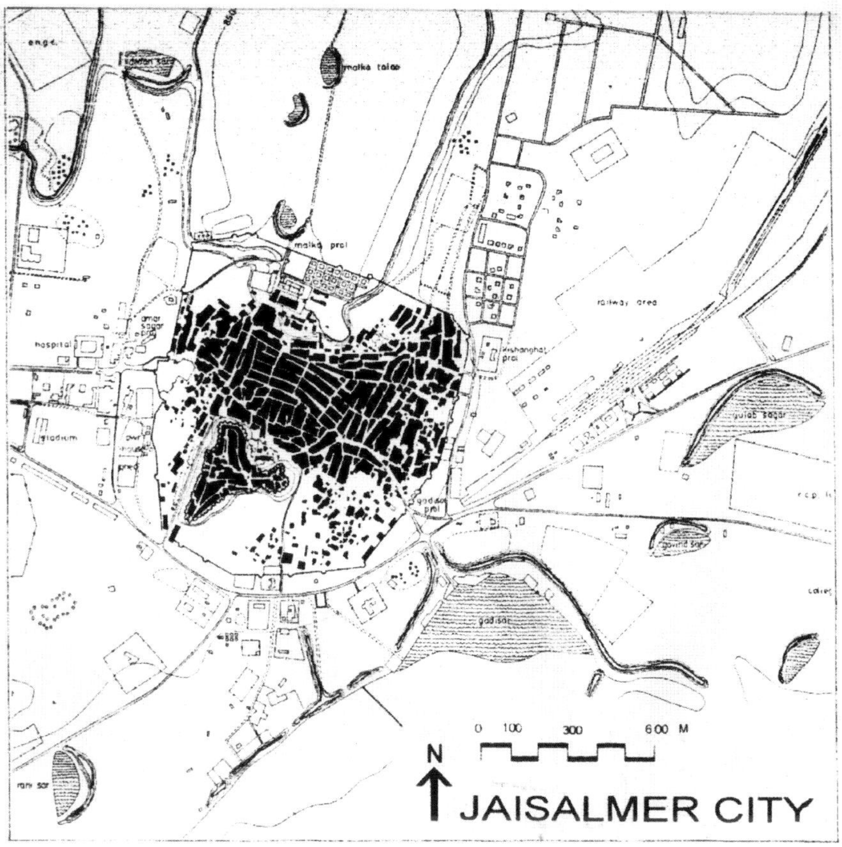

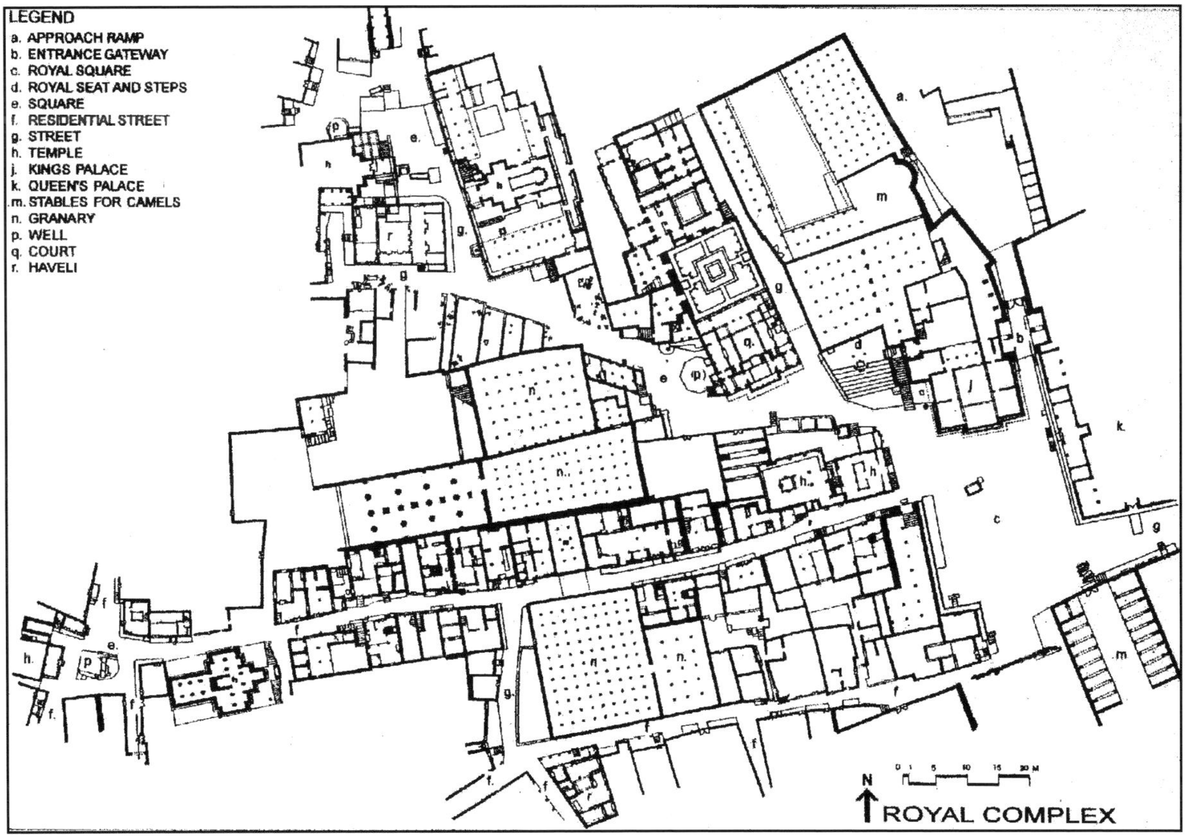

Jaisalmer Fort, Citadel, Palaces and Temples

To enter the fort, one passes through the massive Sūraj Pol, and then Gaṇeśa Pol and Hawā Pol, the entrance to the citadel. Beyond the tunnel of the gate is the Palace Square with many buildings around there constructed during the sixteenth-nineteenth centuries. While each building is independent, they are built so close to each other to form a mass. They were built probably in the following order: the oldest is Zenānā Mahal (sixteenth-seventeenth century), then Sarvottam Vilās (during the reign of Akhai Singh, CE 1722-62), Raṅg Mahal (during the reign of Mūlarāj II, CE 1762-1820), Motī Mahal (CE 1813 or later than Gaj Vilās), and Gaj Vilās (during the reign of Gaj Singh, 1820-46), the most attractive building among the structures in the Fort. The lowest part of Gaj Vilās is the massive plain wall, but intricate *chatrī* (bowers) are placed at regular intervals to go up with more *chatrī* works giving an elegant look to the building. Though the final form we see now is the renovated one of the nineteenth century, but this period (sixteenth-seventeenth) centuries, was really the high time of Jaisalmer, reflecting the intense trade activities and the political solidarity of the time. The building activities developed as the time went by, and the total city planning was not necessarily applied as in the case of the contemporary Islamic cities.

After the middle of the nineteenth century, when Jaisalmer became a protectorate of the British Empire since 1818, European influence became apparent in the buildings reflecting the new lifestyle, but not to the extent of other cities of the time. The new palaces like the Bādal Vilās and Jawāhar Vilās were constructed in the lower city near Amar Sāgar Pol. While the former was built by the Muslim craftsmen, the latter was constructed for the use of the British Resident in the "Indo-Saracenic" style, showing the interesting amalgamation of various architectural styles, but essentially retaining the traditional style of Rajasthan, typical to Jaisalmer.

Besides the royal palaces, we can see many temples in the fort, mostly Jain temples. Rulers of Jaisalmer were Hindus, but they were the great patrons of Jainism, and the Jains also, rich and active traders, were the patrons for the rulers enjoying various priorities in turn. Jain culture made a striking progress during the reign based on these temples. Along with their gorgeous mansions called *havelī*s, several beautiful temples were constructed and numerous images were placed in the temples [Jain 1972: 371-78]. The typical examples may be seen in the eight Jain temples within the fort.

Seven of them are constructed to form a mass together [*fig.* 1.5]. There are some different theories as for the date of construction of these temples but obviously, the oldest among these temples is Pārśvanāth, built in 1416 or 1417 by Seth Jaisingh. The second oldest is the Sambhavanāth temple constructed in 1432 (or 1420). This temple is known to have its own *Jñānabhaṇḍār* or the Library-cum-Research Centre of Jainism, established in 1443 by Jinabhadra, and has ever since served for the development of Jain culture. Manuscripts housed here are 3,000 in number, 500 among them are written on palm leaves. The oldest manuscripts among them go back to as early as the eleventh century including the Jain and the Buddhist *sūtra*s, and some of them are the earliest evidences of the locally made handmade paper in the fourteenth century.

Other Jain temples are Candraprabhu Svāmī, Aṣṭhapaṭha or Kuntunāth, Ṛśabhadeva (Ṛśabhanāth), Śāntināth, and Śītalanāth in the probable order of construction. Only Mahāvīra Svāmī Temple stands a little apart from this group but belongs to the same period. As for the date of construction of each, there are some different theories, but it is certain that they have been constructed within a period of 130 years or so, between CE 1417-1547. It was really the high time of the Jain culture and the overall art and culture of Jaisalmer. In order to clarify the chronological sequence and the complicated relationships between the temples so closely built in a cluster, Kamiya [1995] has painstakingly surveyed the temples [*fig.* 1.5]. The temples have rich carvings in their architraves, parapets, porches and *śikhara*s (pointed spire), all elegant and graceful. The greatest attraction of these temples is the *toraṇa,* viz. gate built on a pair of decorated columns in front of the entrance of Pārśvanāth temple. The columns are ornamented with lotus flowers, animals, *makara*, etc., and adorned with lively sculptures of gods and *apsaras* in graceful motion.

19: Camels and the keepers participating in the event with festive fervour. Garish colour of camels' ornaments along with the tingling sound of the bells add gaiety and gala to the festive mood of the event. (next page)

Havelī: The Typical Mansions of Jaisalmer

The typical architectural style in Jaisalmer can be best seen in the structure of mansions called *havelī*s, facing each other along the streets [*fig.* 1.6]. They are thin and tall buildings, generally more than two-three storeys, built so close to each other as if they form a single

20

20: A camel coming out of Sūraj Pol, the tall and massive gate of the Fort. (facing page)

21: Intricately designed balcony with latticed windows of the present Royal Palace, Bā Vilās, in the city (popularly called "City Palace") outside the Fort. The exquisite craftsmanship of carved *jālī* (trellis) or *bāṛī* (opening across the stone wall-panels) is noteworthy and is also applied for the mansions and *havelī*s.

22: Majestic façade of the Royal Palace or City Palace outside the Fort, fully decorated with the most intricate stone-carvings.

21

22

23: Balcony of Raṇvīr Singh-kī-Havelī outside the Fort. Jain merchants competed with each other to construct some gorgeous mansions or *havelī*s in the city.

24: Paṭvoṅ-kī-Havelī, belonging to the rich Jain merchant, Guman Chand Paṭvā. Beautifully decorated windows and balconies give a mesmerising light-and-shadow effect to the buildings and streets around. (facing page)

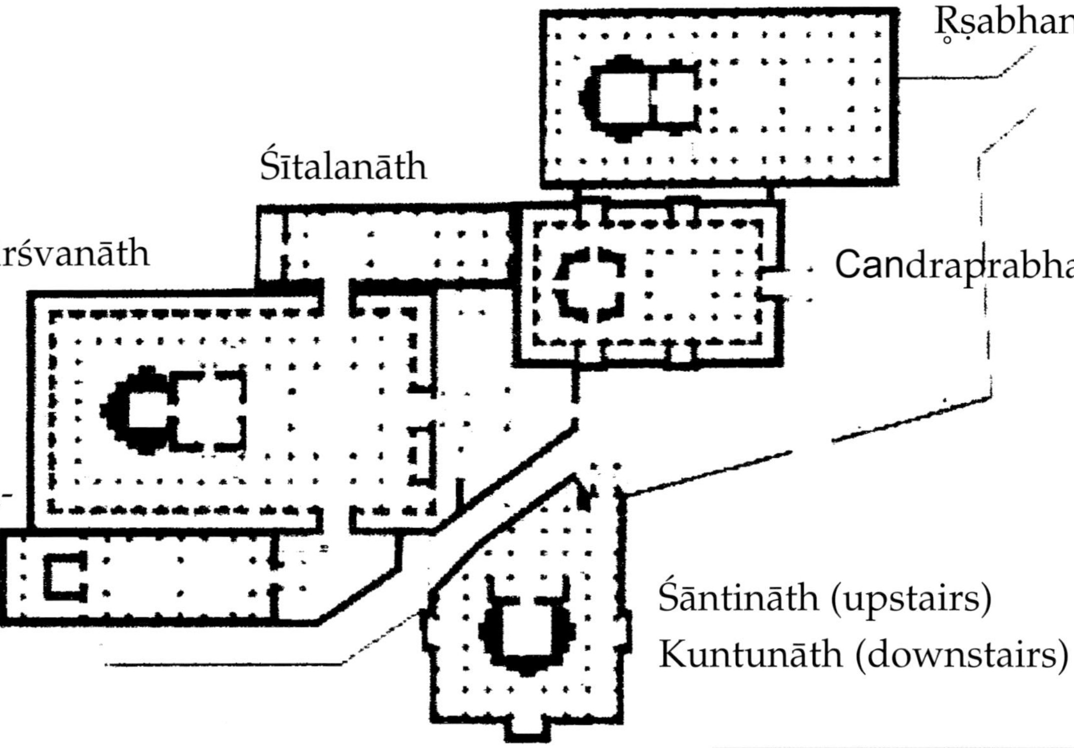

fig. 1.5 Jain temples within the Jaisalmer Fort [Kamiya 1995].

integral cluster but each house is in fact independent. As time went by, the expanding family had to build new rooms upwards due to the limited space. Frontage of a house is narrow but depth is quite long, usually providing a well-style courtyard in the middle for the light and ventilation. The courtyard is the meeting centre for the family, an important space for the extended family. It is an open space inwards but closed to the outsiders, a typical feature in this part of India. An open space to communicate with the others is the platform called *oṭā* in front of each house, thus serving as a buffer zone between the private and public. Below the *oṭā* is a semi-underground space generally used as a store or a depot, and steps going up lead to the entrance of the house [*fig.* 1.7].

Most of these *havelī* houses are built with carved stones piled up one by one, but the essential structure is followed by that of the wooden architecture, using the vertical pillars and horizontal lintels, holding the façade walls with projecting *jharokhā* as well as the beautifully carved bay-windows and intricate *chatrī*.

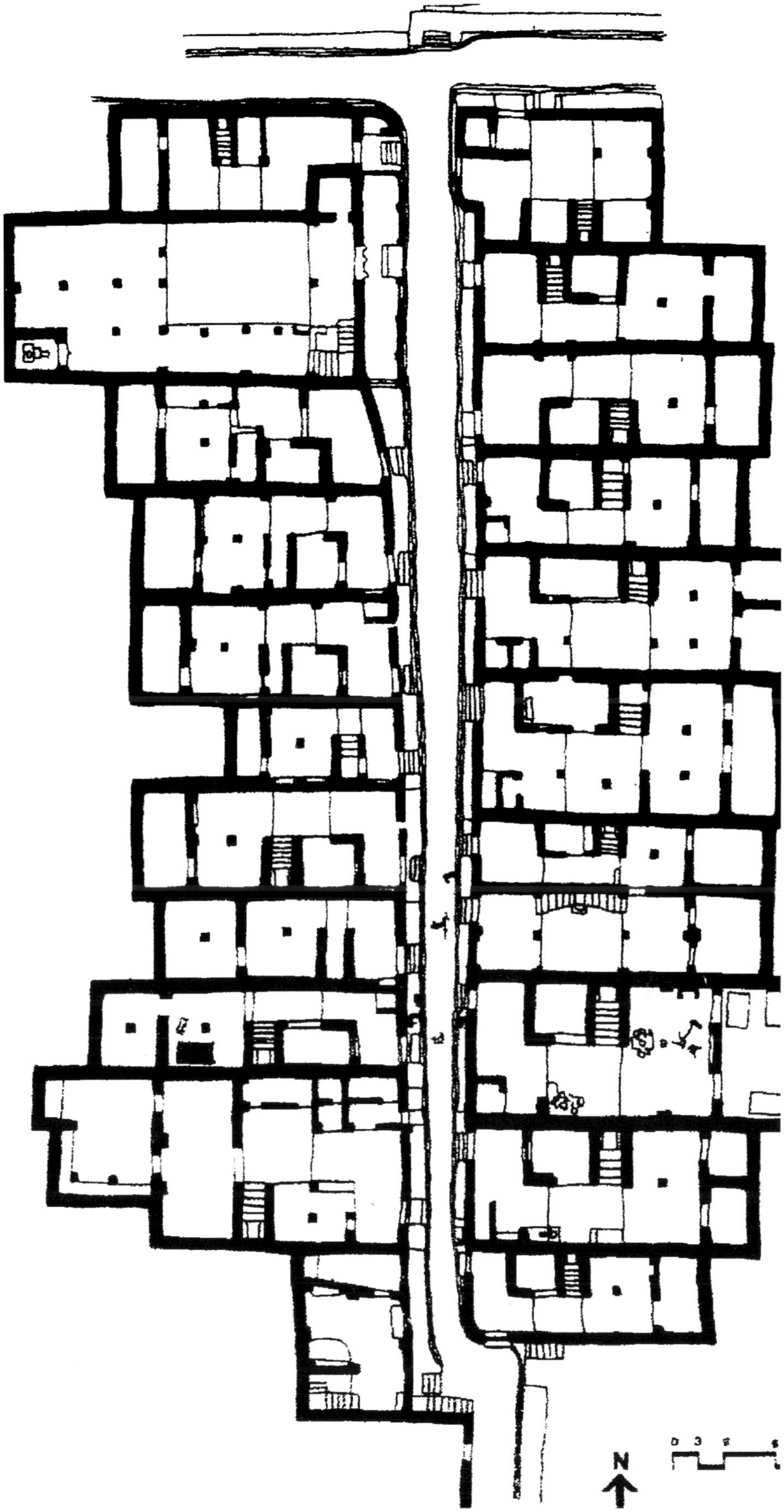

fig. 1.6: A street in Jaisalmer dotted with *havelī* [Jain & Jain 1994].

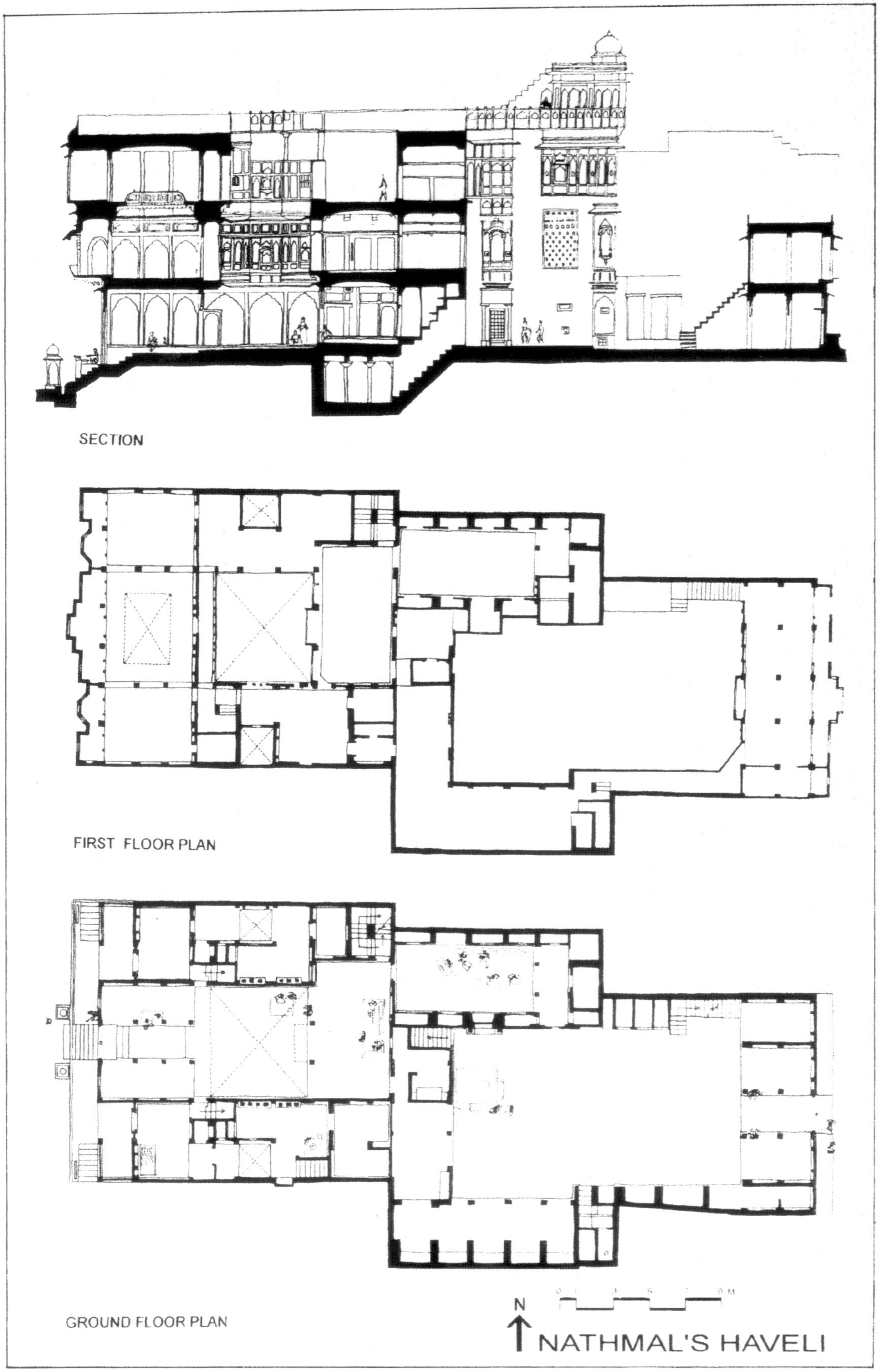
SECTION
FIRST FLOOR PLAN
GROUND FLOOR PLAN
N
NATHMAL'S HAVELI

Projecting balconies and bowers at regular intervals frequently use corbel vault and not the true arch, and the picturesque façades go up high to reach the roof. They are further carved intricately with *jālī* (trellis) and other minute and complex geometric patterns and one would take them as wooden structures, but they are in fact all carved out of the sandstone slabs — the technology is simply superb.

Such architectural style can also be seen in the mediaeval mansions in Gujarat. Trellis was popular as it was quite convenient for the ladies behind *pardāh* to peep at the outside world through the limited openings, and was adopted by many families, both Hindu and Muslim in the West and the North India. Probably most of the panels with trellis used for balconies and bowers were pre-fabricated, and popularly utilized at the time of extension or the repairing works. The best example of such magnificent *havelī* may be that of the Paṭvā family (*Paṭvoṅ-kī-Havelī*), the oldest and the largest, built in *c.* 1805 CE for the five sons of Paṭvā Gumān Chand, a Jain, in five storeys with as many as 66 *jharokhā*s. Edges of the eaves of the bowers hang down as if to represent the thatched roof of a Bengali farmhouse, and thus called Bāṅglā style, that was also so popularly adopted in the Mughal architecture as we see in Delhi and Agra. Though the inhabitants were the Hindus or Jains, the buildings they lived in had been so much influenced by the Muslim (more particularly the Mughal) architectural style.

A few more prominent *havelī* examples of Jaisalmer are Dīvān Nāthmal-kī-Havelī, built in 1885 for the *waẓīr*. It is also five-storeyed with 40 rooms. The architects are said to have been the Muslim brothers, Hati and Lālū. The *havelī* for Dīvān Salīm Singh, built in 1815 is also noteworthy. It is so high as if to compete with the royal buildings or the kingship proper. It is also popularly called Jahāẓ Mahal (Boat Palace) as the top of it looks as if floating in the sky [see the relevant plates].

Smaller houses of the commoners in the city of Jaisalmer are simpler and not more than two-storeyed high, but follow the basic plan and structure of the other bigger houses or mansions, possibly due to the limitation of space within the city or the fort. Many families live in bastions or by the side of the city walls partly utilizing the existing massive stone walls, forming a sort of labyrinth. Many of them are still made of mud blocks, and it is pleasant to see that

fig. 1.7 Nāthmal's famous multi-storeyed *havelī* [Jain & Jain 1994]. (facing page)

25-27: Balconies and windows of *Paṭvoṅ-kī-Havelī*. Strong contrast of light and shadow is the charm of these heritage buildings. Some balconies and windows were meant only for the ladies to peep the outside world through them.

29

30

28: Dīvān Nāthmal-kī-Havelī that once belonged to Hati and Lālū brothers, is one of the best *havelī* architectures of the city. The inner courtyard is in an open-well style and is wide enough to invite the sun and fresh air.

29: Carved balconies and windows of Dīvān Nāthmal-kī-Havelī. The upper rooms, particularly with smaller windows, were meant to keep the privacy of the inhabitants, especially of the ladies.

30: Details of an elephant carved on a lower wall of Dīvān Nāthmal-kī-Havelī. Carved within a frame of intricate design, together with the decorated saddle and the pad of the elephant, it shines like a richly embroidered brocade.

often the walls are painted in white, red and yellow. However, houses of the people who follow more or less a nomadic lifestyle in the desert, the house plan is totally different. Plan of the mud house in an irregular square plan is thatched and shows a remnant of the building tradition of the area since prehistoric time. We can well see that the desert life persists through the ages by the stout people living therein.

Some Important Places in and around the City

Besides the palaces in the fort and the city or *havelīs* in old quarters of the lower city, there are many important and interesting places to see within and in the outskirts of the city [*fig.* 1.8]. Loḍarvā, 16 km north-west from the city on the banks of the Kak River, is the former capital of the kingdom before Jaisalmer, dating back to the middle of the twelfth century. The beautiful city once with Jain and Hindu temples was destroyed by the Ghorī in 1191-92 but was beautifully restored back by Tharu Shah, a rich trader of *ghee*, in 1617. Loḍarvā still remains as a centre of pilgrimage for the Jains, and Pārśvanāth Temple is one of the most important temples here; the beautifully carved *toraṇa* in front of it and an artificial bronze model of *kalpavṛkṣa* or the legendry tree grown in the heaven are really the masterpieces by the craftsmen of the time [*Pls.* 39-41]. The main icon is made of white marble, and diamond is said to have been studded on the head. Invasions and attacks launched by the Muslims were meant essentially for the enormous wealth that was stored in the temples, and not necessarily because of the pagan faith of the attacked.

Another important site to see is the Garisar Lake, which has served as the major source of water, or of the life of the citizens. In fact, there are many *sāgar*s (tanks), artificial or natural, around the city meant for the everyday use and irrigation, but Garisar Lake just outside the city gate is the nearest and the most important among them. Unique buildings around the lake, including the Tiloṅ-kī-Pol or the "prostitutes' gateway" so called according to an interesting legend, and some more *chatrī*s add beauty to the serene scenery. Other tanks with natural beauty along with the historical temples and buildings around the city are Amar Sāgar (5 km away) with Jain temples and royal palaces built in 1692, Mūl Sāgar (7 km away) and several other wells, some of which are stepped, or are excavated for bathing and other purposes.

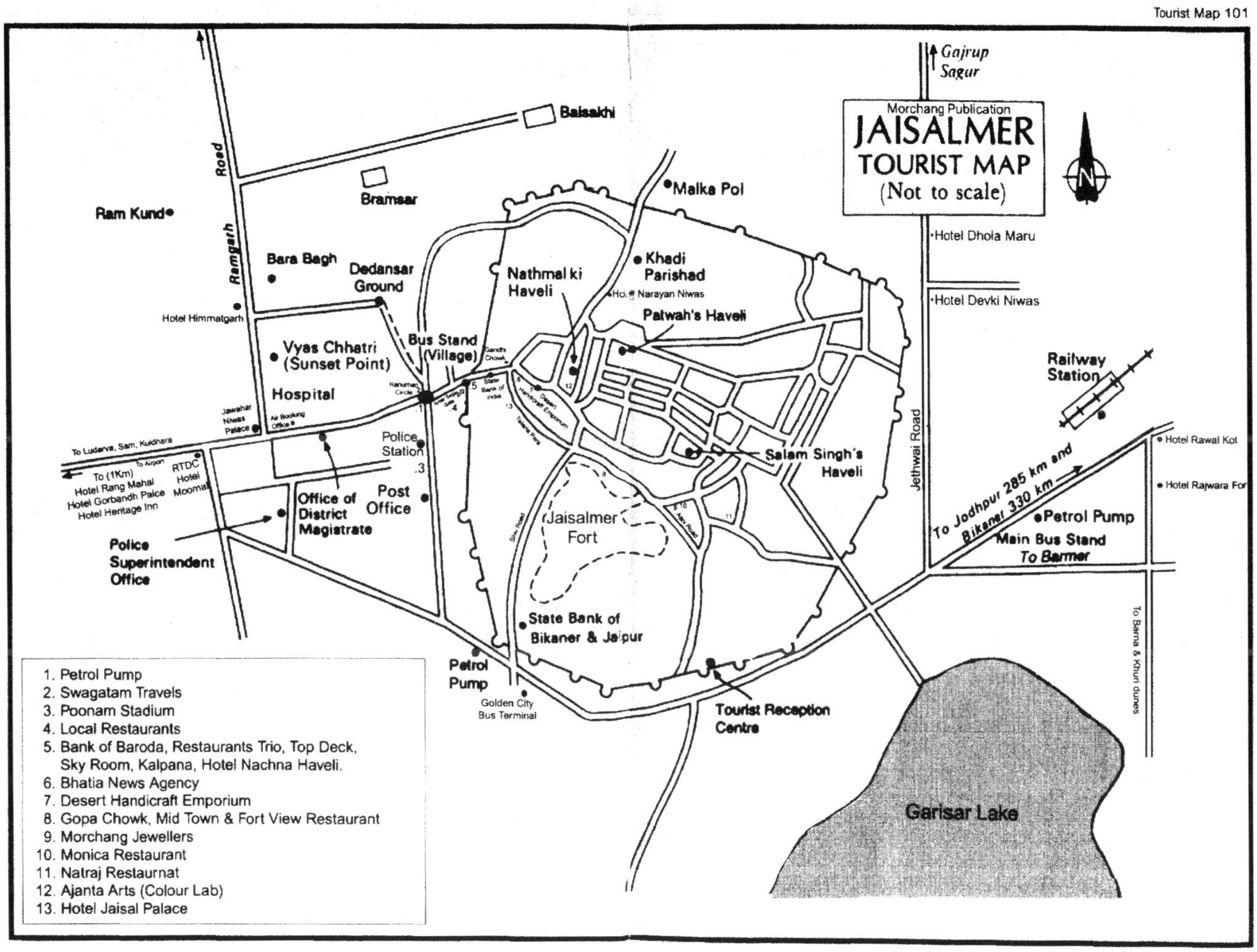

fig. 1.8 Tourist Map of Jaisalmer [Khatri 2001].

31: The topmost storey of Motī Mahal or Salīm Singh-kī-Havelī. The Mohtā family members to which Salīm Singh belonged, used to be the ministers of the Rāval (Rājā) of Jaisalmer. The family was so rich that it controlled even the Rāvals' funds. Extravagance of this building is a testimony to this, but a *rāval*, on being insisted to settle the debts immediately, beheaded Salīm Singh's father, and the son took revenge by managing to become the *dīvān* or prime minister and insidiously took over the power of the royal family and ran the state. However, he too was murdered and his descendants emigrated to other lands, leaving this splendid *havelī* vacant.

32

33

34

35

32: Jaisalmer Fort seen from Salīm Singh-kī-Havelī reveals and reflects the dramatic history of the city royal.

33: A massive *havelī* built in stout symmetry for an extended family. The lane in front of it is so narrow that a particular fish-eye lens had to be used here to photograph.

34: A cluster of the Jain temples with eight temples inside the Fort including Śrī Cintāmaṇi Pārśvanāth Mandir, the oldest (consecrated in 1416) and the most important among them. The other temples are Sambhavanāth, Śītalānāth, Śāntināth, Kunthunāth, Candraprabhu, R̥ṣabhadeva and Mahāvīra Mandir.

35: Sculpture on the wall of a Jain temple within the Fort. The posture of a lady (*apsaras* or *nāyikā*) looking into a mirror, is a typical pose in the mediaeval Rājpūt style, but the lower limbs are stylized and lack in spontaneity as compared with the Khajurāho examples of the Candella dynasty in the twelfth century Bundelkhaṇḍ.

While these ponds and wells represent the sources of peoples' life, there is a huge necropolis representing the netherland. Generally speaking, a cemetery may not be a tourist attraction but Bāḍābāgh (Big Park) here is something else. This is a very wide cemetery ground with many *chatrī*s that look Islamic at a glance, but in fact, they are the funeral monuments or *samādhi*s of the Hindu *rājā*s or aristocrats along with those of their wives who had committed *johar* or self- immolation to become *satī* (the faithful).

Even certain Hindu saints could be also cremated and commemorated in this type of a *samādhi*, against a popular belief that the Hindus would have no tombs. Domes and arches of the *chatrī* here are so formed by corbelling, and not by adopting the true arch. This is a unique amalgamation of different cultural traditions that have bloomed in the desert. We can really feel the history of the city and the heroes here. There are also the picturesque gardens and ponds around, and a temple dedicated to a folk deity Khetrapāl, to whom people offer prayers for harmony and peace of the family. *Vyās Chatrī* or the "Sunset Point" is not too far from here, where one would see the breathtaking scene of the sunset, instantly painting the whole city in crimson red.

Jaisalmer as the Cultural Centre: Religion, Art and Literature

There is much more to be mentioned about the rich cultural heritage of Jaisalmer; for instance, the sculptures that decorate the temples and the secular buildings. While many of the Jain sculptures of Jaisalmer date after the fifteenth-sixteenth centuries, some of the idols are older than the years of construction of the temples as they were brought from Loḍarvā and other places, even from as far as Gujarat, and installed here. Besides the Jain *tīrthaṅkara* images, female figures in various poses and other Hindu images have been also carved out of stones, but they are much stylized and lack in flexibility if we compare them with the twelfth-thirteenth-century examples of Khajurāho and Koṇārka sculpture.

Painting also has not developed so much here, either in the form of wall paintings as we see in Śekhāvatī and Jaipur, or the miniature paintings as in other places in Rajasthan and Punjab, though we do see some interesting late ninteenth-century examples of wall paintings in the Raṅg Mahal of the Palace showing the European influence. The earlier examples may be seen in the murals of Paṭvā

36: Sculptures of dancers and musicians in rhythmical postures, with a standing figure of Pārśvanāth, the 23rd *tīrthaṅkar*, in a recess. (previous page)

(*Paṭvoṅ-kī-Havelī*) or Ṛśabhanāth Temple, probably painted by the Jaipurī fresco and mural painters as in other parts of Rajasthan in the early nineteenth century [Agrawala 1979: chap. V; Jawahar Kala Kendra 1998: 75-78].

The skill of art in Jaisalmer culminates rather in architecture and carpentry, carving out the intricate geometric designs throughout the walls, pillars and lintels, etc. or projecting *jharokhā* and *chatrī*. Besides the stone and woodcarvings for architecture and everyday utensils, some other handicrafts have also developed over the years [Pal 1984]. Textile dyeing by resist-printing or tie-and-dye using indigo and alizarin are well known. Weaving and embroidery of carpet and felt are also very popular trades. Silver, metal and stone jewellery works, as well as ivory, lacquer and leather works add further colours to their life. The best example may be the colourful saddle of camel, so richly decorated by the owners and highly praised even in their folk songs.

As we have seen, Jaisalmer is so rich and diverse with its varied cultural traditions and heritages, and deserves to be known in more depth. In fact, it has actually come to attain the international fame once again more recently, and has become a popular spot for the tourists, both foreign and domestic. This is not at all a new phenomenon in her great history. Jaisalmer has been a city in the oasis serving for so long as an active centre-point for the trade of silk, spices, indigo and opium, with the countries like Persia, Iraq, Arabia, Egypt, and even as far as some African and the European countries ever since its establishment. Foreign caravans used to take ample rest here and even paid quite an amount as toll tax, benefitting the budget of the city. Richly decorated *vilā*s or palaces and *havelī*-mansions still vividly tell the glorious story. Besides the actual trade of merchandise, caravans exchanged ideas and information to enrich the respective cultures of the destination lands. The local traders, however, had to vacate their homes for more than half a year, but left behind them many lovely songs, ballads and oral literature of parting, expressing love to their family and homeland. These are still sung by the local bards, the Māṅganiyār, to the lively rhythm of *ḍholak* and *kartāl*.

With a little setback in the eighteenth-nineteenth centuries, Jaisalmer rose once again and came to life with her rich cultural heritage, attracting the tourists and visitors now even from the lands far away. Conservation and preservation works of historical

37: Mother and child, sculpture of the Jain Temple of Pārśvanāth at Loḍarvā near Jaisalmer, representing a late Rājpūt sculptural style. Besides Vaiṣṇavism, Jainism was very popular in Loḍarvā, and in about CE 1034, a noted saint of the creed Jineśvarsūri, a pupil of Vardhāmansūri, visited this town and his two sons, Śrīdhara and Rājadhara, constructed this temple. The temple might have been destroyed by the invader Muḥammad Ghorī, but was fully repaired later in CE 1618-20. (next page)

38: Dancing *apsaras* or *nāyikā* in the Jain Temple of Pārśvanāth at Loḍarvā. Though stylized, dancing posture in the typical three-bent *tribhaṅga* is quite charming. (next page)

37

39

40

41

39: The Jain Temple of Pārśvanāth at Loḍarvā. The intricately designed façade is the hallmark of craftsmanship. The architectural style is generally of the eleventh century, but is unique in that the lower half is in the south Indian style, whereas the upper portion represents the north-western style of architecture.

40: An aesthetic backside view of the temple is as wondrous as the façade.

41: *Kalpavṛkṣa*, or the legendry "Heavenly Tree" said to be growing in the Paradise of Gods to bestow any wishes, is installed here behind the Jain Temple of Lord Pārśvanāth at Loḍarvā. It is a unique piece of bronze craftsmanship, and one of the main attractions for the pilgrims, both Hindus and Jains.

42: The main idol of the 23rd Tīrthaṅkar Pārśvanāth sitting in *siṁhāsana* posture, now enshrined within the Jain Temple at Loḍarvā. It was reinstalled here in the early seventeenth century after the original main idol belonging to the mid-eleventh century was transferred as the main deity of the Jain temple — Śrī Cintāmaṇi Pārśvanāth Mandir — within the Fort of Jaisalmer.

42

43: Garisar Tank, one of the most important water-sources for the city, with a beautiful *chatrī* or bower in the Islamic style at the centre. It was constructed by Mahārāval Jaisal in CE 1156 and renovated in CE 1367 by Garsi Singh, from whom its name is derived. Water of the tank used to dry up during the dry seasons till 1965, when the water came to be supplied from a tube well some 15 kms away. Water now comes from the Indira Gandhi Canal since 1993.

44

45

46

44: An overview of the Garisar Tank along with some historical structures as seen from the Fort. The picturesque and pleasant scene presents a contrast to the dry atmosphere of the city, with no gardens and greens, unlike the other Islamic cities of the time.

45: Tīloṅ-kī-pol or Garisar Gate stands at one side of the Tank nearer to the Fort. Tiloṅ was a harlot from Hyderabad, Sindh, but as a memorial of her birthplace she spent here lot of her wealth to construct this beautiful gate at the entrance of the lake. However, as the legend goes, the Rājā and his family felt reluctant to pass under the gate donated by such a type of lady. Tilon then got an image of Satyanārāyaṇa installed on top of the gate, to bestow a Vaiṣṇava touch on it.

46: Cenotaphs built in *chatrī* style in Bāḍābāgh, an interesting combination of the Islamic cupola-domes and the Hindu-style pillars, though many of the domes still retain the older pre-Islamic corbelled character. In spite of the general belief that the Hindus do not build tombs, such commemorative cenotaphs have been quite commonly built for the heroic *rājās* or saints of merit on the cremation spot, *samādhi*, since the mediaeval times.

47: Hero stone with *satī* figure enshrined under a funeral *chatrī* to commemorate the self immolation of a virtuous widow who threw herself into the funeral pyre of the dead husband. While such faithfulness is highly praised, especially among the Rājpūts, there could have been also an intention to pacify the rancorous spirit caused by the tragic death.

47

48

49

buildings have been carefully carried out also by the archaeologists and architects together with the modern technology besides other renovations, but not in a way as to disturb the authenticity of their basic concepts and the cultural and spiritual traditions.

With its serene and the beautiful monumental heritage and its sparkling living culture, the "Golden City" Jaisalmer would shine once again with her unparalleled glorious history, rich culture and great traditions nurtured through the ages by the brave people, the descendants of the proud but hospitable Rājpūts.

48: A lone figure of Lord Hanumān looks over the vast desert-land, once packed with many houses. There are still traces of old flourishing villages inhabited by the Pālīvāl brāhmaṇs, but they were evacuated during the severe oppression of Salīm Singh, *dīvān* of Mūla Rāja II, some 200 years ago. (facing page)

49: Deserted houses in ruin inside the Fort. They require quick and careful conservation and restoration as they form and represent the important cultural and historical aspects of the city, but are unfortunately neglected to decay. (facing page)

50: A camel being taken around the foot of the Fort. Camel is a very useful multi-tasked animal in this arid land and a good companion of the locals. Jaisalmer has traditionally been a famous camel-breeding centre for ages.

51: Jaisalmer Fort, towering above the arid ground — as seen from south-west. Ladies in front are in typical Rājasthānī dresses, comprising tight bodice called *kudai kāñchlī*, long frilled *lehṅgā* or *ghāgarā* skirt and *oḍhanī* scarf-shawl. They also don heavy sets of thick armlets. (next page)

50

2

Village Life of the Thār Desert

Kodai Konishi

If you happen to visit Jaisalmer for the first time and not being familiar with the desert world, and simply start roaming about the vast arid land there, you might feel that there's nothing to see or enjoy other than the barren and sterile wasteland all around you. It may look like a scene of the "end of the world", where the dried up ground extends immeasurably with the sporadic small and big sand dunes or a few camels here and there — a typical monotonous desert scene.

However, if this very world becomes a familiar sight for you, and if you come to visit the desert repeatedly encountering the immense diversity of lives of the inhabitants, you would realize that your first impression of the desert was quite wrong. You might gradually come to know how the people of the Thār Desert have strong coherent networks connecting scattered households, and how the diminutive shrines perched in the shade of trees or rocks have all rich stories behind them. Besides, the many rites, rituals and performances held in each household or community reflect the profound historical and cultural background of the Thār Desert. This is a short description of the socio-cultural depth of the desert world, which I could myself observe during my long and short stays in the Thār Desert for over fifteen years, especially around Jaisalmer.

The Living Site

Broadly speaking, there are two kinds of residential formation of the people in the desert. One is called *gāon*, in which various "caste groups" and "tribes" live together, forming comparatively a large residential site which we may call as "village". Example is shown in [*fig.* 2.1], Barnā village in the southern part of the district.

The other habitation is kind of a "hamlet", consisting of plural households scattered around in the desert, called *dhanī*. Basically, *dhanī* is formed by several households of a single descent group, sometimes containing a dozen of houses gathered in one place. Basically, *dhanī* consists of a number of single social group such as "caste" or "tribe", and it sometimes expands to a village-like residential area, consisting of dozens of households. *Gāon* and *dhanī* are scattered generally in clusters in barren spaces, each of them being a separate entity. However, these clusters have thick interlinks with each other irrespective of the long distances.

52: A freshly painted local house of mud-blocks inside the Fort. Sun-dried bricks or mud blocks adopted here are as hard as stone, and the fringes of doors, windows or stairs are often decorated white with lime against the red background. The cool courtyard is the centre of domestic activities, particularly of the ladies and children. (previous page)

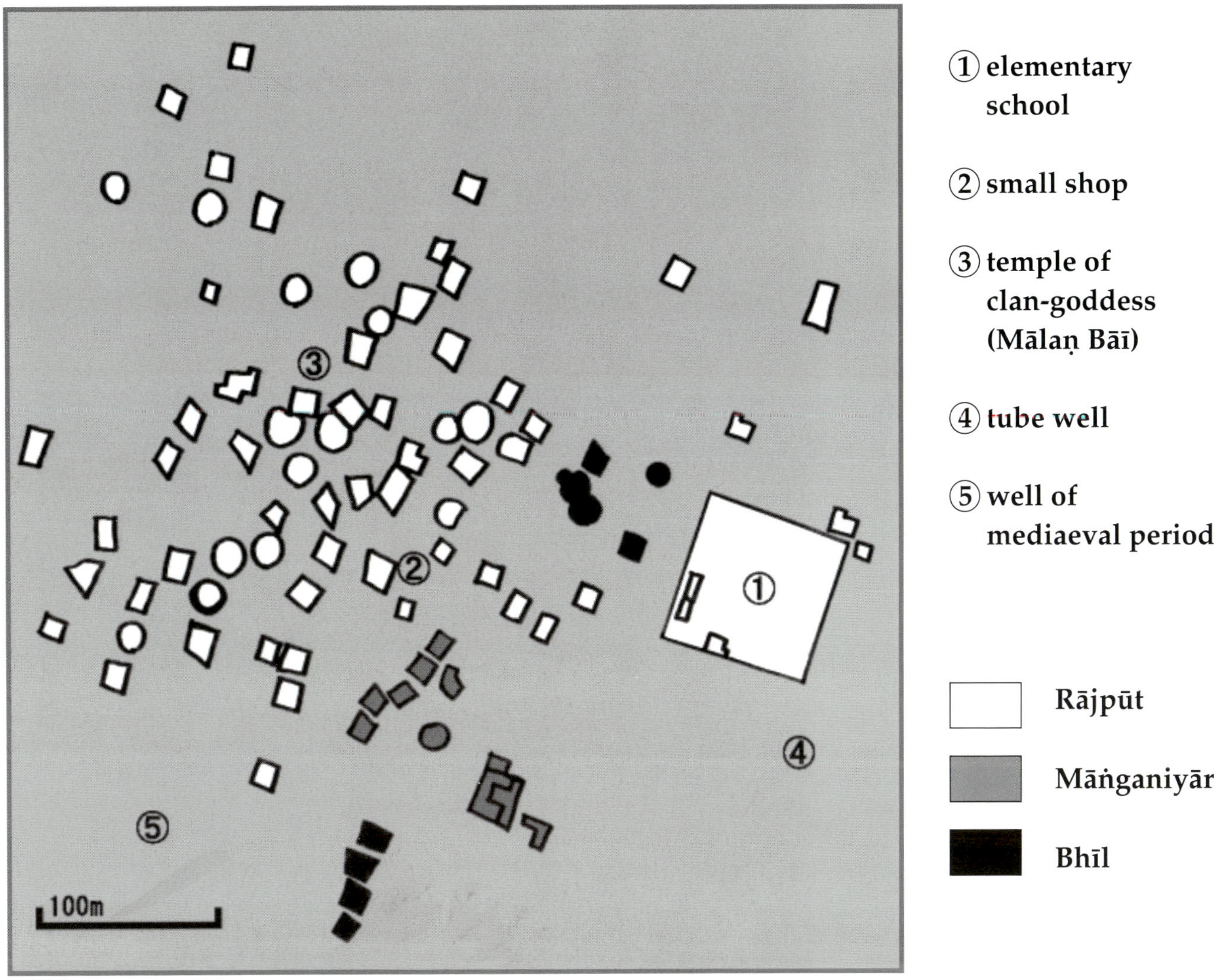

fig. 2.1: Distribution of Houses in Barnā village.

This style of habitation is well reflected by their mode of production. Most of the people in the desert, irrespective of their traditional occupations, own tiny pieces of land for cultivation of miscellaneous cereals such as *bājrā* (*Pennisetum glaucum*) or *jowār* (sorghum), and tend to settle down near the field itself. At the same time, as they are pastoralists, they need widespread bushy areas to feed their livestock such as camels, cows, goats, sheep, and so on.

Table 2.1: Demographic Statistics of Rajasthan and Jaisalmer District (2011)

	Total	Male	Female	Growth rate in % 2001–2011	Sex Ratio of female per 1000 men	Density per sq. km.
Rajasthan (State)	68,621,012	35,620,086	33,000,926	21.44%	926	201
Jaisalmer (Dist.)	672,008	363,346	308,662	32.22%	849	17

53: The Fort and a cow in dignity. Even a cow looks brave enough and heroic in this historical city, especially with massive and solid bastions in the background.

54: A cow passing through a narrow shady lane within the Fort. A girl is trying to offer a piece of *capātī* (pancake) from a small window of an old house.

Surprisingly, nearly 85 per cent of the people in Jaisalmer district are living in the desert and leading such a style of life. They are half agriculturists and half pastoralists, keeping their traditional occupations intact.

Social Structure in Villages

Generally, large-scale residential area such as "village" was built deliberately by the descendants of the warrior caste or the Rājpūts, a long time ago. Rājpūts are recognized as descent groups of several kingdoms that constituted Rājpūtānā (older name of Rajasthan) since the early mediaeval time. Therefore, these villages are named by using the particular ancestral names of the lineage to which the inhabitants belonged, which are also used as their ramified clan names. Once these different clans of Rājpūts located their residential places in the desert, they called for the people of plural service groups to settle in the same area to serve or work for them. These service groups included the daily workers, such as barbers, weavers, potters, craftsmen, carpenters or leather workers, as well as those involved in rituals, such as musical instrumentalists, singers, genealogists, dancers or clowneries, etc.

55: A fierce-looking bull in a lane within the Fort scares away the children. Still men and domesticated animals live together peacefully in their everyday life. (below)

56: A newly wed couple with attendants coming down from a *havelī* in the lower city. Both ends of the *oḍhnī* or shawls of the couple are tightly tied together, and the bridal attire is so colourful in contrast to the pure white *sārī* of the bridesmaid. Auspicious red handprints adorn the wall and door of the *havelī*. (facing page)

57

58

59

57: A lady painting the auspicious symbols at a house of the newly weds. Against the background of bright red-ochre smeared over the beige mud walls, geometric and symbolic signs are drawn in white, but they are not decorated abundantly with big paintings of human figures or animals like those seen in Śekhāvatī and other historical cities in Rajasthan. Such ritualistic wall paintings are called *ṭhāpe* in south-east Mewar.

58: Auspicious symbols like *svastika*, sun and trees are painted by the ladies on the doorway to welcome the newly wed couple. These signs of fertility and prosperity may also form the important components of the ritualistic floor-paintings generally called *māṇḍanā* in Rajasthan.

59: Ladies gathered for the wedding ceremony sitting closely together under the picture of the beautifully painted Gaṇeśa, who would remove any obstacles and bring in luck. Menfolk might have gone to the edge of village to receive the groom's party, or might be gathering in a separate room on this occasion, but they never mix with the womens' group.

60: Pounding dough to make the sweets for selling in the local *bāẓār*. As the man is busy working in the airy street, a lady draped in typical Rājasthānī attire passes by.

61: Various types of snacks and sweets like *jalebī* are readily made and sold off. While the main local dish is generally very hot and spicy, people also love sweets, sometimes too sweet.

62: Selling jaggery or unrefined black-sugar by weight. The thick jaggery is prepared by boiling down the sugar cane juice. It is very sweet and nutritious.

61

62

63: *Lohār* or blacksmith at work, using the leather bellows operated by his daughter. People still prefer the handmade cutlery and farming tools made in this traditional way to the manufactured readymade tools sold in bigger *bāẓārs*. (facing page)

64: Collecting wool to spin. Wool has been an important trading item of this region, and is essential for the local people as well, not only for the winter-wear but also for the summer dress too to shutter the heat if dry. (facing page)

63

64

65

66

65-68: Old-men reading newspapers, either in English, Hindi, Urdu or Gujarati, reflecting the variety of the linguistic groups within the population. Literacy rate is quite high in the city especially among the Jain community, as they have always been quite keen on education.

67

68

These service-giving groups are called *kisbī* or *kasabī* in general. They provide many kinds of service to the Rājpūt clans, and in return, Rājpūts reward them by paying them in cash or giving them certain share of the crop or the cattle for their services. Usually, this service-and-reward structure is called "*jajmānī* system" in social anthropology of India, but the situation here is slightly different. The structure of this relationship in Jaisalmer certainly contains the hierarchical connotation as the patron-client order as is seen in the other rural areas of India, but it also comprises a sort of egalitarianism. In the villages of the Thār, the groups composing the structure are connected to each other by sharing a common ethno-historic origin with religious narratives, which function to make them share the cosmology and strengthen the ties of every group, including the Rājpūts and other service castes. Therefore, the village structure observed here is Rājpūt-centric, but at the same time, the ideology of social relationship is egalitarianistic in nature, because the ideology relates the different societies with each other in the historic and religious horizon, regardless of the social groups they actually belong to.

Here is an example. In the southern part of Jaisalmer District, there is a clan of Rājpūts who claim themselves to be the descendants of the Paramāra kingship, which prospered in the West India during the mediaeval ages. Their clan name is Sodhā, and they reside in the southern part of Jaisalmer especially around Barnā village which is located in the north of Khūrī village, a famed tourist spot of the desert. They worship a *kul-devī* (clan-goddess) called Mālaṇ Bāī, a daughter of Berisār who existed as a legendary king of the Paramāra-armlet kingdom. Similarly, as in other Rājpūt clans, they have a title (*nakh*). Sodhā clan's *nakh* is Paramār, which is drawn from the historical kingship of Paramāra. Therefore, they sometimes call themselves "Sodhā-Paramār" in high pride, connecting their clan name and historical title which is otherwise generally hidden.

In addition, there are other social groups whose titles are Parmār around the area. Such groups also worship the same clan-goddess (Mālaṇ Bāī) as Sodhā Rājpūts. Actually, these groups are traditionally regarded as *kisbī* or *kasabī*, the service groups like the Bhīl (soldiers, watchmen), Māṅganiyār (musicians, genealogists), Kālberiyā (snake charmers, dancers), Meghwāl (leather workers), Suthār or Suntar (carpentars), and so on. These groups are ideologically connected by sharing the historical origin (*nakh*) and the belief for transcendental being (*kul-devī*). Involved in the Paramār-family, these groups are firmly connected, keeping tight relationship with each other. Yet, if these groups encounter with the other (non-Paramār) Rājpūts, the relation would turn to be more hierarchical.

69: Decorated dolls on display used for the string-puppetry in Rajasthan called *kaṭhputlī*, the most well-known and probably the oldest form of puppets in India. Themes of puppetry range from mythological to historical, but the battle scenes of the heroic Rājpūt *rājā*s like Pṛthvīrāj Cauhān, or the court scenes with beautiful courtesans playing ball-game, are popular and frequently shown.

Religious Life

The most important aspect of religious life of the people of Thār is the "clan- god called *kul-dev,* or goddess called *kul-devī*". There are various clans that are historically connected by several ancestries of Rājpūt family, and each clan has its faith in a particular god or goddess. For example, Bhāṭī Rājpūts, the clan of the founder-rulers of Jaisalmer kingdom, mainly worship the goddess named Taṇoṭ Rāi or Taṇoṭ Mātā, who has been enshrined near the Pakistan border. This Mātā or the Mother-Goddess is said even to have protected the Rājpūt soldiers from the bomb attacks by the Pakistan Army during the Indo-Pakistan War in 1971. While these clan-originated supreme beings are worshipped as the guardian deities of specific clans, these

70: Manipulation of string dolls of *kaṭhputlī* from behind the back curtain. The dolls are manipulated from above, held by four-six strings tied in a prop, and the puppeteer's figure remains concealed behind the frontal curtain. The lower half of the curtain forms the stage, opens in the shape of a series of arches, suggesting a palace.

71: An old-fashioned postbox fixed to a wall of the Fort is almost buried under the piles of puppet dolls for sale. Bassi, a small town near Chittorgarh, used to be the centre of production of such dolls or wooden toys, but are now abundantly made and sold in tourist centres like Jaipur, Udaipur and Jaisalmer.

72: Puppet dolls and other items are also sold as souvenirs on the roadside. As the puppet shows are gradually getting less popular among the local people, if not for the tourists, the puppet dolls are becoming the popular commercial merchandise nowadays. (facing page)

71

70

72

deities also function as the historical tokens of legitimacy of social groups. Each deity has rich legends, myths or heroic stories behind, and the people of the desert proudly sing or narrate these stories from time to time.

These deities are worshipped during major festivals twice a year in special months. On these occasions people gather together, even coming from afar outside the district to celebrate the special day with other devotees. Usually, these festivals are accompanied with rituals and sacrifice of specific species of livestock, such as goats or water buffaloes. The huge gathering of people shares the happy time and food, and try to recognize their roots and thus identify each other.

The great deal of shrines of gods or goddesses called *thārī* are found all around the desert. Some of them are petty shrines of clan-deities, but others are sometimes difficult to be identified even by the inhabitants here. Most of them are local goddesses, and these *devī*s are generally grouped or classified altogether as "seven sisters", called *Sāt Bahin* (an example is shown in Table 2.2), or "sixty-four *jogan*", called *cauṅsaṭh jogṇe* (*yoginī*) in Mārwāṛī language.

Table 2.2: An Example of the set of Devī of 'Seven Sisters'

1.	Tanoṭ Rāi
2.	Temde Rāi
3.	Deg Rāi
4.	Kāle Ḍuṅgar Rāi
5.	Svargia Rāi
6.	Ghantiali Rāi
7.	Aināth Rāi

The Seven Sisters have a brother called Khetpāl-jī and the most important sacred place for this deity is located at Bāī Bāgh. These local goddesses, classified in these groups, are equivocally named by people depending on the place and time, therefore the confusing controversy regarding the naming and grouping of the goddesses often takes place among the people, and the desert then becomes almost like the packed abode of the goddesses.

Besides the diversity of the Supreme Being being scattered around whole of the desert, another important aspect of the peoples' religious life is the ancestor worship. The society in the Thār Desert consists of patrilineal descent-groups, therefore, the people may be able to recite a dozen of paternal ancestors' names. Also, the musician caste, such as the Māṅganiyār, plays a role of keeping the patron's paternal genealogy. Some of these ancestors would turn to be a kind of deities, namely *petrik*, and their spirits could be enshrined in a small altar inside the residential space. Other ancestors called *bhāmiyā* or *bhomiyo* would float around the villages, and they must be hospitably worshipped outside the house. If the offerings with proper religious rites to the *bhāmiyā* are forgotten, some kind of misfortune might befall the household. Whether the ancestor would become a *petrik* or a *bhāmiyā*, it is said that the result depends on their nature and actions when they were alive.

Table 2.3: Order of the deities placed in the rites of marriage celebration

Name of the God/Goddess	Classification
Mālaṇ Bāī	Clan Goddess (*kul-devī*)
Pābūjī	Hero God (*jhūjhārjī*)
Temde Rāi	A Goddess among the "Seven Sisters"
Bhuriyā Bābā	God of Samādhi
Kāle Dūṅgar Rāi	64 *jogan* (*cauṅsaṭh jogṇe*)
Dokarā Pañcā Pīr	Ancestral God (a Muslim Saint)
Dharmā Dādā	Ancestral God (*petrik*)
Takrā Bā	Ancestral God (*petrik*)
Mūla Dādī	Ancestral God (*petrik*)
Indarā Dādī	Ancestral Goddess (*petrik*)

Table 2.3 shows an order of local deities worshipped in the rite of marriage celebration at a household near Koṭhḍī village, demonstrating how the beliefs of the local people are complicated and mixed up with various elements. It contains Hindu gods or local goddesses and even the Muslim saints.

Besides these local deities typically seen in the desert area, the people here also worship the "authentic" Hindu gods which are seen all over India. For example, Bhāṭī Rājpūts, the ruling family of the Rājpūts in Jaisalmer, trace their origin to the Yādava clan, the famed

73: Morning *bāẓār* of fresh vegetables on a busy road in the Lower City. Farmers prefer to bring in their agricultural produce to the busy corner of the town, rather than going to the institutionalized market, such as the one at Gopa Chowk near the gate.

74

75

clan of the popular Hindu god Kṛṣṇa (Krishna). Therefore, Kṛṣṇa is an important genius for them along with their clan goddess, Taṇoṭ Mātā.

In various rites and rituals seen around urban or rural area, most of the rites must be started by praying and giving offerings to Lord Gaṇeśa, the popular Hindu god with the elephant-head. After the marriage ceremony, the family of the groom would paint the figure of Lord Gaṇeśa on the wall of their house to show the neighbours that the ceremony was held successfully [see *Pl.* 58].

Although there seems to be a sort of division between the "authentic" Hindu gods and the local deities in the religious life of the people, it is like a textile woven with the diverse elements of faith. For instance, we can understand the situation by taking up the case of *Gaṅgaur*, the women's festival observed in Rajasthan. The main character of this festival is Gaurī Mātā who is considered to be quite an ancient figure, rooted in the pre-Aryan worship of Mother Goddess. Girls and ladies carry the figure of the goddess, in a large procession from the Palace Mandir in the middle of the city up to Garisar Tank, the mediaeval reservoir at the outskirts of the city. Allegedly, this festival mainly means celebration of the advent of monsoon, or a special prayer for the growth and well-being of the girls. Besides these local traditions, sometimes Gaurī Mātā would be identified as Pārvatī, the spouse of Śiva, the exponent figure of the Hindu pantheon. In this way, only one event or rite taken up for study would reveal the manifold meanings therein.

Fairs and Festivals

It might be a common situation seen all over India, irrespective of where they live, that the people here celebrate numerous festivals throughout the year to enjoy and release the feelings of gloom of daily life. Some festivals are observed within the households or clans to remember and serve their ancestral gods or clan-gods, while the other festivals are quite large-scaled ones with the huge gatherings of people from far and wide, beyond the district or the state. Above all, the Rāmdevra Fair is very famous for the tremendous gathering of devotees it attracts from all over the country, particularly from the North India as well as the South.

This fair is held for eleven days during August and September at Rāmdeva Village, 11 km from Pokharan station in Jaisalmer District. Bābā Rāmdevjī, the local god enshrined in the village is said to have

74: Fresh vegetables being sold in the morning *bāẓār*. They are dewy-fresh and cheaper than in the regular markets, and as they are sold by women, it is easier for the ladies to go there and buy. (previous page)

75: A lady buyer eagerly negotiating the price. It is also a part of the joy of shopping. Alluring are the colourful wall paintings of a *havelī* behind the vegetable stall. (previous page)

76: Mother and child from some village in a typical and colourful attire sitting cosily in a corner at the morning fair. Noticeable are the heavy sets of armlets, origin of which dates back to the days of Moheṅjo-Dāṛo civilization, some 5,000 years ago! (previous page)

fig. 2.2: Bābā Rāmdevjī as drawn in a poster.

been a very brave Rājpūt warrior in the fourteenth century, who devoted all his life for the upliftment of the marginalized or those victimized by the invaders [*fig.* 2.2]. He is also famous as a saint, having achieved that status during his lifetime. It is quite interesting to note that Bābā Rāmdevjī is also worshipped by the Muslims, as this legendary warrior is also famed as an Islamic saint or *pīr* at the same time. There are widely narrated stories about the origin of this phenomenon. It is said that one day, five Muslim saints visited Rāmdevjī to defeat him by testing his supernatural powers but in vain. When they saw the unrolled miracles of this Rājpūt warrior before their very own eyes, the five saints had to prostrate themselves before Rāmdevjī. As this anecdote spread over the area, various Muslim people started to worship this powerful saint and called him "Rām Shāh Pīr".

Besides this kind of large-scale fête featured by the pilgrimage, there are quite a few modern festivals of tourist interest. Every year in the month of February, Jaisalmer has a gala event called the "Desert Festival". It is said that this festival attracts more than 25,000 tourists from within and outside the country. We would be excited then by various performing arts, such as folk dances [*Pl.* 91], musical sessions, acrobats, and so on. There are also many other fascinating events organized on the occasion, namely camel polo [*Pl*s. 88, 89], moustache contest [*Pl*s. 92, 93] and other unique contests.

The festivals that are observed all over India, such as the Holī, Dīwālī (Dīpāvalī), Daśahrā (Dussehra), etc. are also cerebrated here in the desert city, but rather in a quite localized way. For example, the Holī in the desert area is started by children with sticks in their hands. They go to the garbage place (*akudi*) with the sound of hitting the sticks of each other and shouting the phrase as below:

> Laying down, water buffalo, the field, growing water melon, papaya,
>
> Children eating, this much! This much!!"

This yell suggests the peoples' wish to be healthy and wealthy. The fire is lit then on the sticks after the childrens' return, that burns away the inauspiciousness of the previous year and welcomes the hopeful New Year.

Diversity of Religions

So far we have roamed only around the Hindu side of the desert world. However, the religious aspects of Jaisalmer are actually woven together deeply with multiple elements. First of all, we should remember that Jaisalmer had been an important relay point of the East-West trade route, and this mediaeval city was opened out to the Western Islamic world such as Sindh or Afghanistan. This historical factor made Jaisalmer to receive and retain much of the Islamic influence since then. Around Garisar Tank [*Pl*s. 43-45], we can find the Muslim graveyard expanding to the outskirts of the citadel. All day long, we can hear the echo of *aẓān* calling the devout Muslims for prayers at the mosque or *masjid*. Muslim population rate of Jaisalmer district is approximately 25 per cent of the total, the rate being quite higher than the countrywide rate of the Muslim population which is about 14 per cent.

Like Bābā Rāmdevjī as we saw above, we can find Islamic (especially *sūfī*) traces around the city and in the midst of the desert where the mausoleum-shrines of Islamic saints called *dargāh* are dispersed from place to place. Some folk music groups such as

Laṅghā and Māṅganiyār are, as we will see later, the followers of the Sunnī sect of Islam. Especially Māṅganiyār have a unique character about religious life. Though they are Muslims, they have been serving only for the Hindu patrons with their music. Sometimes they help *bhopī*, the witch doctors of the desert possessed by the local Hindu goddesses. It is also their important role to praise the clan-gods or goddesses of patrons. As such, we easily could find local Hindu aspects within their religious life. We should not look at them with the bias of a Hindu/Muslim dichotomy, or we may get confused to understand their diverse religious life. Hindu or Muslim is not an absolute classification here to define the people.

For the Jains also, Jaisalmer has been quite an important centre of pilgrimage. One of the most important Jain temples was founded well inside the residential area of the citadel. These temples are dedicated to the prominent Jain saints, namely Pārśvanāth, Sambhavanāth, Śāntināth, and so on [*Pl*s. 34-38]. There are also some more important Jain temples far from the city, like Ādiśvara temple in Amar Sāgar, Pārśvanāth Temple in Loḍarvā [*Pl*s. 39-42], Ādināth and Pārśvanāth Temple in Brahmasar, etc. attracting thousands of the Jain pilgrims and the tourists alike.

The World of Folk Art and Performance

The diversity of religious life as we saw above is a result of the historical process, which is featured with "transference" of goods, people and culture, as the city had been the breathing point on the dry and harsh trade route. Since the time when the offsprings of the Yādava established the habitation here as their homeground, Jaisalmer functioned as a wealthy oasis town for the traders, pilgrims, nomadic performers and various other service groups. When we talk about the life-space of Jaisalmer, we cannot leave the problem of "transference". Here we shall enter into the world of nomadic performers, and survey the transference and life of the desert people.

In Rajasthan state, there are two types of Bhopā people. One is a kind of witch-doctors that tell people's fortune when possessed by the spirits of local deities. The other is a performer group that sings and plays musical instrument called *rāvaṇhatthā*. The latter usually play music in front of a long painted cloth screen called *paḍ*, explaining the painted myths of the desert hero gods such as Pābūjī and Devnārāyaṇ [*Pl*. 78]. From season to season, they move within a wide range of Rajashtan. They are said to be living around Jodhpur

77: A Bhopā or story-teller singing local ballads of gods and heroes against the setting sun, while the birds are heading back to their nests in the background. Bhopās in Mewar region are generally engaged in magical rituals, but here in Mārwāṛ, they are essentially bards by profession.

78: Bhopā performing in front of Motī Mahal, Salīm Singh-kī-Havelī. Their songs are purely folkloric and touchy for the local people, but are becoming quite popular nowadays and are even recorded in cassettes and CDs. They are usually accompanied by a child or their wife when performing. (facing page)

79: A Bhopā sings the epic of Pābūjī in front of the painted scroll, *paḍ*. Pābūjī is a legendary local hero who fought against Dodo Sumro, a Sindhi *rājā*, and brought back war booties including camels for the first time. His heroic deeds and the tragic romance are painted in *paḍ* that extends for about 4.5 m in length and 1.5 m in height, in a typical and characteristic painting style of *paḍ*. Story of Pābūji is sung poetically to the accompaniment of *rāvaṇhatthā*, a two-stringed instrument with tiny bells attached on the bow, while no other instruments are generally used. It is a very interesting example of "painting narration" in Rajasthan called *paḍ vāčño* or *vāñcano*. The Bhopā here wears the same costume as Pābūjī in the painting, he being the legendary Pābūjī personified.

and Nagaur districts, but their sphere of activities is beyond these districts, practically all over the Thār.

In Jaisalmer, we can see their way of life a little away from the city behind the citadel, setting up tiny tents there. Nowadays, most of the Bhopā earn their livelihood from the tourists visiting Jaisalmer. Around the fort gate, especially the square called Gopā Cauk, we can see them playing *rāvaṇhatthā* in traditional dress, and trying to sell the instruments or silvery anklets to the visitors [*Pl*s. 77]. In contrast, it is harder to encounter the "traditional" Bhopā, moving away from the city earning a little sum of money from the villagers. They are trying to retain the patronage from the scattered households around the desert, playing instruments and singing various myths of the desert heroes and explaining the painted clothes to the village audiences.

The lady called Bhopī makes a short interlude of the sung story, and with a lantern in her hand, spots the light on the particular part or scene of the painting relevant to the song. The performing art show is usually held at midnight, by gathering local people who are fascinated by the brave stories of the ancient heroes. Bhopās make full use of their own networks to maintain relationships with their patrons, and keep shifting all the way in the desert from season to season.

The case of Māṅganiyār, the Muslim musician community, is interesting for observing their patron-client relationship. An etymology of Māṅganiyār is *māṅgno*, meaning "to beg" or "demand a reward". This word suggests that their occupation is deeply connected with rewards from the patrons. They proudly call their occupation as *maṅgal mukhī*, "the happy sphere" of life. This shows their position and role in social life and in ritual scenario. At the time of rituals, especially at the important "rites of the passage" such as birth, name-giving for the baby and marriage, they play very important roles by singing and playing instruments along with the each programme of the particular rite. Without their performance, the rites or cerebrations cannot be assumed as complete [*Pl*s. 81, 82, 83].

Though their patrons are living only sporadically scattered around the desert and sometimes their residences are quite far beyond the district border, these musical communities keep on recognizing and deciphering as to how many patrons' households are in their charge, and what their latest economic conditions are. This deep connection with patrons has been inherited through generations of social relationship.

Another important role of the musical communities is to

maintain genealogy of the patron's clan. When they visit a patron's house, they would begin chanting the genealogy of the family, and this ritual performance is called *subrāj* or *śubhrāj*. They would also sing devotional songs or *bhajan* for the local deities, especially for the clan goddesses relating to the patron's lineage.

Roles of the musical community show how important it is to maintain and extend their relationship with the existing patrons. In contrast, the caste of snake-charmers, Kālberiā, does not have such deep and fixed relationship with their patrons. They move from city to city or village to village, performing their skills and attracting the locals. It is the male's performance to fascinate audience with a "dancing" cobra, playing traditional wind instrument, *pūṅgī* or *bīn* [Pl. 80]. However, the dance is generally performed by the female. They wear colourful skirts with a broad hem, decorating their traditional dress with gaudy ornaments. Sometimes the male Kālberiā play *pūṅgī* and *ḍholak* (percussion instrument), and the ladies get into the rhythm, turning round with their skirt fluttering. Above all, the group dance called *indonī*, which is performed by several ladies forming a circle, is the most famous one [*Pl.* 91]. These performances are held occasionally, and they move from place to place where festivals or rituals would take place.

The above description gives only a few examples of various performing communities in the Thār. Their modes of movement and earnings are diverse. Bhopās move from a particular base to another seasonally, whereas Māṅganiyārs fix their base in a village and commute between patrons' houses, beyond the district border. Kālberiā roam around the desert looking for the place where the people need them in the rituals. In the touristic context, these performer groups tend to be described under a single category of "gypsy" as a whole, but their way of living, and meanings of their performing arts are deeply embedded in the various social settings of Rajasthan, that we shall have to study more minutely in detail in their proper socio-religious contexts.

Changing Mode of Life: Towards Modernization

Growing influence of modernization of the Jaisalmer city have begun to change the life of the local villagers. People have stopped shifting their residence frequently and have started to settle down at one place. Though people still visit each other frequently, their mode of transport has changed from camel to motorbike. Even in the midst of

80: An old Laṅghā musician playing *Sindhī sāraṅgī*, a typical musical instrument for them. They also play another type of *sāraṅgī* called *Gujarātī sāraṅgī*. They are a group of folk musicians generally living in Jodhpur area, and are famed along with another well-known group of bards called Māṅganiyār living in and around Jaisalmer. (next page)

81: Kālbeliā or a *jāti* (community) of snake-charmers playing *murlī* or *pūṅgī* made of gourd shell. Snakes move their heads to and fro or right and left following the movement of *murlī*, and not to the sound of music in fact. They wander from place to place like the other itinerant groups of people such as *jogīs*, also putting up acrobatic performances on request. (next page)

81

the desert, villagers can easily communicate with the world outside with the mobile-phones. Electrified houses are quickly increasing.

In such a changing situation, people have started trying to fit their traditional occupations to be applied to the modern needs and industrial structure, and are even looking around to be engaged in the increasing service jobs. Then, what about the desert performers? They tend to prefer getting cash from the tourists in the city rather than small rewards from the patrons. This tendency has made them to live in colonies inside the city, such as Kalākār Colony near the Central Bus Stand. Moreover, some of the musical performers are playing an active role in the global music scene. They often play in concerts in the European and other countries, and CDs and DVDs are produced in plenty. Their passports are, in fact, full of immigration stamps of the foreign countries.

The social relationship based upon a system of patronage has been collapsing in such a process of modernization. However, the cosmology and the world view of the desert people, grown in the vast expanse of arid soil and sand, along with the beliefs in the various local deities, have still been taking the deep and sound roots there, to form and retain the peculiar identity of "Jaisalmerī". Though the strong connections of the performers with their patrons are gradually vanishing, the relationships within their own caste or kin groups have been getting strengthened, showing the vigorous trends of cooperation with each other to live and let live in the harsh nature, and the hard social conditions of this quickly modernizing world.

82

82: Music ensemble by the Māṅganiyār with *kamaycha* (string instrument with round body derived originally from Iran), *khartāl*, *morchaṅg* and harmonium. Songs are sung in solo and in unison, then passing the phases one after the other, resulting in thrilling improvisations within certain rhythmic and melody frames of *tāla* and *rāga* as in classical music.

83: A Māṅganiyār boy playing *khartāl* or castanets, a typical percussion instrument to produce a lively rhythm, together with the two-sided drums, *ḍhol* and *ḍholak*. However, *khartāl* is not used by the Laṅghā even for the same repertoire of songs.

84: *Morchaṅg* or Jew's harp, another important instrument for the Māṅganiyār. Jew's harp is a unique instrument in the cultural history of world music due to its wide distribution. It is also used in Baluchistan and Afghanistan by the name of *chāṅg*, and in south India, in classical rhythm ensemble, by the name of *morsiṅg* as a percussion instrument.

85: Acrobatic dance performance *terāthālī* by the ladies, accompanied by rhythmic instruments. They carry water-pots of brass on their heads while dancing vigorously even on the blades of swords, or hit many tiny cymbals tied in line on their legs by throwing the other pairs of cymbals tied by strings on their wrists and fingers to the rhythm.

83

84

85

86: *Mīrāsī* or court musicians, playing in front of Paṭvoṅ-kī-Havelī. Formerly, *rājā* and courtesans, or rich merchants used to be their patrons, but now they have to play for the general public, not unlike the case of Māṅganiyār, and the latter, in turn, are assuming the more prestigious name of *mīrāsī* in the recent times.

87: Exciting camel race is one of the major events of the Desert Festival. Handsome rewards and honours are bestowed on the winners.

88

88: Colourfully decorated camels gathering at the venue along with their riders for participation in the annual Desert Festival in winter. (facing page)

89: A little boy and a girl dressed gorgeously as Rājkumār (prince) and Rājkumārī (princess) on a decorated camel with an embroidered colourful saddle.

90: Procession of camels is a big attraction of the Desert Festival. Even tourists may have a chance to take a ride on the camels.

89

90

91

91-92: Rājasthānī belles performing folk dance at the Festival.

93: Heroes of the moustache contest. Thick moustaches and long beard are the signs of manliness and pride of the Rājpūts.

94: Winner of the moustache contest. The thin and long colourful turban dyed in *bandhanī* style or tie-and-dye, worn by the winner, is a prestigious status symbol of a man.

92

93

94

95

95: Śrī Karṇa Rām Bhīl, once a Guinness record holder as the longest moustache-bearer and an excellent *nād* player. *Nād* is an end-blown long flute with four holes only and is quite difficult to play, but Karṇa Rām could play it constantly without taking any breathing breaks; even singing simultaneously while playing *nād*.

96: Karṇa Rām was also a fierce folk dancer, but he is no more as his tragic and violent end came in 1985 with his murder due to the prolonged hostility of his sworn enemies. These are the rare images taken during his lifetime in his last years. (facing page)

RAJASTHAN

97: Traditional weaver of a nearby village working at a simple loom. The striped cotton with alternating dark blue and white or red vertical stripes is called *sussī* and is used mainly for women's gathered pants, *śalvār*. It is also commonly woven in Sindh (Pakistan).

98: Grain container and a stone rotary quern in a village house. The Rectangular storage bin made of clay for storing the grain is called *causar*. The outer surface is decorated by applying extra clay for making interesting intricate designs. Similar clay bins can also be found in Kacch (Kutch) in Gujarat.

99: Potter's wheel and painted pottery in a corner of a potter's workshop. India has not generally developed glazed pottery, but blue-glazed pots have been significantly made in Rajasthan, showing some resemblance with the products in Hala, Hyderabad, Sindh. Round pots with wider mouth are called *maṭkās* and are used for storing water, and those with smaller mouth are called *ghaṛā* and are used for carrying water.

98

99

100

101

102

100: A woman potter painting a pot. Bi-chrome geometric designs, painted in black and red over the buff background, are again similar to the samples from the pre- and proto-historic sites of Punjab and Sindh in Pakistan, with centuries-old long tradition. This type of the larger pot, with an open wide mouth, is called *bilaunā* and is used for churning milk, a lid is attached to preserve the contents.

101: A potter beating the side of a *maṭkā* while still wet with a paddle to shape. Generally the bigger-sized vessels are made by coiling the thinner clay bands, then scraped to shape and beaten by a paddle. Even the pots thrown on the wheel may be further beaten with a paddle to give the final shape as required.

102: Piled-up unglazed *maṭkās* for sale near the city bus-stand. Most of them are without any decorations as they are purely utilitarian. The painted pot varieties again show similarities in colour and design with those from the adjoining districts in Pakistan, and are even comparable with the prehistoric or early historic pottery of the region.

103: Selecting the right water-pot or *ghaṛā* of the desired size. It is one of the essential routines of their desert life to carry and store water. Mouth of a *ghaṛā* is not wide open like a cooking vessel called *hāṇḍī*. Water kept inside a *maṭkā* cools down slowly as it slowly seeps out through the unglazed surface of the pot and reduces the temperature inside by vapourization.

104: Temporary but a pathetic parting scene before the long-distance bus journey. In such a busy crossroad of trading routes as Jaisalmer, there might be so many such parting scenes, though such an occasion of a wife leaving the village may be rather exceptional. There still are such dramatic scenes, even in a seemingly monotonous life of the remotest villages.

105: "How far should I walk in the desert with a child and a goat?" — It is really a tedious journey through the hot and dry desert land, often across the barren and huge sand dunes. Goat is a good companion in such settings.

106: A packed local bus bound for other towns and villages. People rather prefer to travel on the open roof as it is more airy, but the wind could be even hotter than it is inside.

105

106

107: Womenfolk fetching water from the Garisar Tank. Although it is an artificial source of water, it is really an oasis for this dry city.

108-109: Women carrying water to their homes. Brass or clay, water-pots full of water are quite heavy, but the ladies manage to keep the balance so well. These are the typical scenes throughout Rajasthan.

110: Small but a very precious water-source for the Khūrī villagers in the desert, really the spring of life in the midst of a burning desert land.

112

111: A long way to fetch water. Even a large *oḍhnī* may not be well enough to guard against the strong rays and dry, scorching heat. (facing page)

112: A woman tending sheep in the village, giving water to the young ones. They are as dear to her as her own children.

113: Proud village ladies who may not conceal their faces. The so-called *pardāh* system to confine them in *zenānā* or women's room deep within the house is the custom generally seen among the urban Rājpūts and Muslims.

113

114

115

114: Bridegroom with a sword on the day of his marriage at Khūrī village. Decorated turban and the festoon make the groom look so salient in front of the newly painted doorways with auspicious symbols.

115: Preparing for the marriage ceremony. *Ghee* is being put in a lamp to keep it ready for the nights of happy ceremonial events ahead.

116: Women hiding their faces during the mourning period, but not necessarily wearing black or white mourning clothes.

117
118

119

117: Cow shares a beautifully decorated room with the villagers.

118: Camel is not only a close friend in the desert but also a fortune.

119: Well decorated post office of the village. It is also a place to gather and gossip for the elders.

120: A group of women proceeding for a funeral at Khūrī village. Lady's attire is however as colourful as usual or as at any other festive occasion, and the children accompanying them are also in colourful clothes.

121: Village elders discussing the village matters or exchanging views, sitting on a verandah.

122: Thatched round mud houses are called *bhuṅgā*s, and the whole premises for an extended family is enclosed by a sturdy fence. Houses are set around the open courtyard facing each other. This type of round plan houses can be found more in Kacch (Kutch) and Gujarat, and the origin can be traced back even to the prehistoric time of this area.

123: Kitchen with huge round storage jars bearing auspicious signs like *svastika* and sun symbols, painted with white pigment fringed by red.

122

123

124-125: A lone journey through a huge sand dune of Sam, 44 km west of Jaisalmer.

126: End of a journey.

Glossary

apsaras	heavenly maidens.
aẓān	call for the Muslims to pray in the mosque.
bāḍī	river bed, generally dry.
bāgh	garden or a park.
bājrā	a kind of millets, *Pennisetum glaucum*.
bāṛī	opening across the stone wall-panel.
bandhanī/bandhnī	tie-and-dye, an intricate method of dyeing clothes.
bāẓār	local market, set permanently or semi-parmanently.
bhajan	devotional songs of the Hindus.
Bhāmiyā/bhomiyo	ancestors' spirit floating around the desert thus to be pacified.
Bhāṭī Rājpūt	the ruling class of Jaisalmer.
Bhīl	powerful 'tribal' caste of soldiers or watchmen.
Bhopā	story-tellers/singers in Mārwāṛ using a big narrative scroll painting called *paḍ*.
bhuṅgā	thatched small houses in round plan.
bilauna	large pot with wide open mouth used for churning the milk.
burj	bastion.
capātī	thin pancake made of wheat flour.
cauk/chawk	square or an open space of a city surrounded by buildings.
causar	rectangular storage bin for grains made of clay.
cauṅsaṭ jogṇe	64 *jogans* or *yoginī;* locally worshipped goddesses.
chatrī	bower, often in Islamic style with curved roof.
dargāh	mausoleum-shrines of the Islamic saints.
dhand	small saline pond or lake in a dry desert.
dhanī	hamlet or a small residential site formed by several households.
ḍhol	a type of horizontal drum played by hand or with a stick.
ḍholak	another type of smaller horizontal drum played by both hands.
dīvān	prime minister.

gajdhar	masons, stone-workers.
gāon	village or the rural residential site, bigger than *dhanī*.
ghāgrā	frilled skirt worn by ladies.
ghaṛā	water-pots in various sizes and shapes.
ghee	clarified butter.
hāṇḍī	cooking pot with open wide mouth.
hāṭ	weekly *bāẓār*.
havelī	mansion(s) of rich families.
indonī	group dance performed by local ladies.
jagrī	unrefined black sugar made by boiling sugar cane juice.
jajmānī	socio-economic system based on contracts between patrons and clients.
jalebī	a kind of sweets fried in oil.
jālī	trellis in the typical Rājasthanī architectural style.
jāti	so-called "caste", or the social group defined by birth.
jharokhā	decorated balcony.
jñānabhaṇḍār	Library-cum-Research Centre of Jainism since mediaeval time.
johar	self-immolation of chaste wives on the death of their husbands.
jowār	a kind of miscellaneous cereals; sorghum.
kalpavṛkṣa	heavenly tree grown in the paradise to bestow the wishes.
kamaycha	string instrument with circular body played with a bow.
Kālbelīa	snake-charmers, also engaged in various other performing arts.
kartāl/khartāl	wooden castanets made of two pairs of clappers.
kaṭ-putlī	string-puppets of Rajasthan.
kisbī/kasabī	mutual contract between patron and client as in *jajmānī* system.
kudai kañchlī	tight bodice used by the Rājasthānī ladies.
kul-dev/kul-devī	clan-gods and goddesses.
kuṇḍa	pond or tank.
Laṅghā	folk musicians living around Jodhpur.
Loḍarvā	former capital of the Bhāṭī Rājpūt before Jaisalmer.

makara — mythical sea animal in composite figure of crocodile, dolphin, elephant, etc.

māṇḍanā — geometric floor paintings for ritualistic purposes.

Māṅganiyār — folk musicians living around Jaisalmer.

Mārwāṛ — former territory of Jodhpur *rājā* in North-west Rajasthan.

maṭkā — round and big pot with wide mouth to store water.

Meghwār — leather workers.

Mewāṛ — former territory of Udaipur *rājā* in South-east Rajasthan.

mīrāsī — court musicians by *jāti.*

morchaṅg/morsiṅg — Jew's harp widely used in South Asia.

murlī/pūṅgī — wind-instrument made of gourd, often used by snake-charmers.

nād — end-blown long flute with four holes only.

nakh — clan title showing their origin in historical context.

nāyikā — beloved mistress, a charming lady leader.

oḍhnī/oḍanī — scarf-shawl worn by ladies.

oṭā — raised platform running along the front portion of a house.

Pābūjī — very popular local devine-hero of this area.

paḍ — painted scroll for story-telling, used by the Bhopā.

paḍ vācño — narrative performing arts, or story-telling based on *paḍ.*

Paramār — A dynasty which prospered in West India during the mediaeval time.

pardāh/purdāh — social custom to seclude ladies behind the curtain (*pardāh*).

parkoṭā — city wall or boundary wall of a city.

Pārśvanāth — 23rd and the last Jain *tīrthaṅkara* before Mahāvīra.

Paṭvā — a rich Jain merchant family who built gorgeous *havelī.*

petrik — ancestral spirit or *pitṛ*, turned to be a deity.

pīr — Islamic (*sūfī*) saint.

pol — massive gateway of the fort.

pūṅgī/bīn — double-reed musical instrument made of a gourd.

rāga — melodic mode or mood as the frame of a music tune.

Rājpūt — literally, "descendants of *rāj*" or a warrior's class, and in wider sense, inhabitants of Rajasthan.

Rājpūtānā	former name of Rajasthan, administrative area during the British Period.
rājkumār/rājkumārī	prince/princess.
rāval	*rājā* or a princely leader in Rajasthan, particularly of Jaisalmer.
rāvaṇhatthā	simple fiddle or string instrument used by the Bhopā.
sār/sāgar	literally "ocean", but denotes a big pond or lake.
samādhi	place of cremation, burial or entombment of a saint or hero.
sāraṅgī	string instrument played with a bow.
Sāt Bahin	"Seven Sisters", a set of the locally worshipped goddesses.
satī	virtuous wife who immolated herself on the death of her husband.
siṁ	a yogic sitting posture with both feet held on thighs.
śikhara	pointed high spire of a temple.
subrāj or *śubhrāj*	ritual performance of Māṅganiyār, chanting the genealogy and eulogy of the patron family.
sunthar/suntar	*suthār* or the carpenters.
sussī	striped cloth woven in Sindh, Gujarat and Rajasthan.
tāla	rhythmic cycle for keeping time with music and dance.
terāthāli	acrobatic dance by a group of ladies.
toraṇa	ornamental gateway to the temples and shrines.
ṭhāpe	ritualistic wall painting particularly in South-east Mewāṛ.
thārī	shrine of the local deities.
ṭībe	sand dune in the Thār.
tīrthaṅkara	founder-preachers of Jainism preceding Mahāvīra Jina, who is supposed to be the last and 24th *tīrthaṅkara*.
tribhaṅga	"three-bent" expression of body seen in a dance posture or in sculpture.
vilās	royal palace.
waẓīr	minister.
zenānā	women's quarter with rooms deep within the house.

Select Bibliography

Anonymous, 1996, *Everyman Guides: Rajasthan*, London: David Campbell Publishers.

Agrawala, Ram Avatar, 1979, *History, Art and Architecture of Jaisalmer*, New Delhi: Agam Kala Prakashan.

Begde, Prabhakar V., 1978, "Forts and their Planning", in his *Ancient and Mediaeval Town-planning in India*, Ch. 8: 81-99, New Delhi: Sagar Publications.

———, 1982, *Forts and Palaces of India*, New Delhi: Sagar Publications.

Bhanavat, Mahendra, 1977, *Rājasthān ke Ṭhāpe*, Udaipur: Bhāratīya Lok-kalā Mandal.

———, (ed.), 1974, *Lok Kalā: Mūlya aur Sandarbha*, Udaipur: Bhāratīya Lok-kalā Mandal.

Bharucha, Rustom, 2003, *Rajasthan: An Oral History*, New Delhi: Penguin Books India.

Bhattacharya, B.C., 1974, *The Jaina Iconography*, rev. ed., Delhi: Motilal Banarsidass.

Bhattacharya, Sachchdananda, 1972, *A Dictionary of Indian History*, rev. ed., Calcutta: University of Calcutta.

Chauhan, B.R., 1967, *A Rajasthan Village*, New Delhi: Vir Publishing House.

Choy, Monique and Sarina Singh, 2002, *Rajasthan; including Delhi and Agra*, Victoria: Lonely Planet Publication.

Cousin, Françoise, 1986, *Tissus Imprimés du Rajasthan*, Paris: Editions L'Harmattan.

Department of Tourism, 1982, *Folk Music of Rajasthan*, Jaipur: Government of Rajasthan.

Erdman, Joan L., 1985, *Patrons and Performers in Rajasthan*, Delhi: Chanakya Publication.

Jain, Kailash Chand, 1972, "Jaisalmer", in his *Ancient Cities and Towns of Rajasthan*, Section C: 371-378, Delhi: Motilal Banarsidass.

Jain, Kulbhushan and Minakshi Jain, 1992, *Mud Architecture of the Indian Desert*, Ahmedabad: AADI Centre.

Jain, Kulbhushan and Minakshi Jain, 1994, *Indian City in the Arid West*, Wien: Institut für Planungsgrundlagen / Ahmedabad: AADI Centre.

Jawahar Kala Kendra, 1998, *Wall Paintings of Rajasthan*, Jaipur: Jawahar Kala Kendra.

Kamiya, Takeo, 1995, "Jaisalmer in the Thar Desert", *AT-Special Issue on Jaisalmer*, (in Jpn.) (http://www.kamitjp/04_jaisalmer/jaisal.html).

Kane, P.V., 1973, *History of Dharmaśāstra*, vol. III (2nd ed.), Poona: Bhandarkar Oriental Research Institute.

Khatri, L.N., 2001, *Jaisalmer: Folklore History and Architecture*, Jaisalmer: Morchang Publication.

Kothari, Komal, 1994, "Musicians for the People: The Manganiyars of Western Rajasthan", in K. Schomer (ed.), *The Idea of Rajasthan*, New Delhi: Manohar.

Kramer, Carol, 1997, *Pottery in Rajasthan: Ethnoarchaeology in Two Indian Cities [Jodhpur and Udaipur]*, Washington and New York: Smithsonian Institution Press.

Majumdar, R.C. (ed.), 1957, "Art [of Rajputana]", by S.K. Saraswati, N.R. Ray et al., in *Struggle for Empire, History and Culture of the Indian People*, vol. 5, ch. 20: passim, Bombay: Bhāratīya Vidyā Bhavan.

Majumdar, R.C., H.C. Raychaudhuri and K. Datta 1953, *An Advanced History of India*, passim, London: Macmillan.

Manchanda, Bindu, 2001, *Jaisalmer: City of Golden Sands and Strange Spirits*, New Delhi: Harper Collins.

Mathur, U.B., 1986, *Folkways of Rajathtan*, Jaipur: Jaipur Printers.

Mishra, R.L., 1985, *The Forts of Rajasthan*, Mandawa: Kutir Prakashan.

Nath Aman and Francis Wacziarg, 1987, *Arts and Crafts of Rajasthan*, Ahmedabad: Mapin Publishing.

Newman, D. & S. Chaudhuri, 2006, *Bards, Ballads and Boundaries*, Oxford: Seafull Books.

Oki, Morihiro & M.A. Konishi, 2001, *Folk Paintings from the Indian Earth*, Tokyo: Mirai-sha.

Oki, Morihiro & M.A. Konishi, 2007, *Unknown India: Ritual Performance and the Crafts*, Tokyo: Seiryu Shuppan.

Paine, Sheila, 2001, *Embroidery from India and Pakistan*, London: The British Museum Press.

Pal, H. Bhisham, 1984, *Handicrafts of Rajasthan*, New Delhi: Publications Division.

Prohit, J.K., 2010, *Jaisalmer Hac*, Jodhpur: Usha Publishing House.

Saksena, Jogendra, 1979, *Art of Rajasthan: Henna and Floor Decorations*, Delhi: Sundeep Prakashan.

Saksena, Jogendra, 1985, *Māṇḍanā: A Folk Art of Rajasthan*, New Delhi: Crafts Museum.

Sharma, Nand Kishore, 1981, *Jaisalmer: The Golden City*, Jaisalmer: Seemant Prakashan (also enlarged and revised ed., n.d.).

Sharma, Nand Kishore, 1997, *Way of Life in Desert*, Jaisalmer: Seemat Prakashan.

Skelton, Robert, 1973, *Rajasthani Temple Hangings of the Krishna Cult*, New York: American Federation of Arts.

Smith, John D., 1991, *The Epic of Pābūjī: A Study, Transcription and Translation*, Cambridge: Cambridge University Press.

Somani, R.V., 1990, *History of Jaisalmer*, Jaipur: Panchaseel Prakashan.

Spate, O.H.K., 1954, "The Aravalllis and Central India", in his *India and Pakistan: A General and Regional Geography*, Ch. 21: 565-95, London: Methuen & Co.

Spate, O.H.K., A.T.A. Learmonth and B.H. Farmer, 1967, "The Aravalllis and Central India", in their *India, Pakistan and Ceylon: The Regions*, ch.21: pp. 611-41, London: Methuen & Co.

Sureshwaranand, 2001, *Art and Architecture of Jaisalmer*, Jodhpur: Books Treasure.

Tillotson, G.H.R., 1987, *The Rajput Palaces: the Development of an Architectural Style 1450-1750*, New Haven: Yale University Press.

Tillotson, Sarah, 1994, *Indian Mansions: A Social History of the Haveli*, Cambridge: The Oleander Press.

Tod, James, 1997 (rep. of 1829), "Annals of Jessulmer" and "Sketch of the Indian Desert", in his *Annals and Antiquities of Rajasthan: or the Central and Western Rajpoot States of India*, vol. 2: pp. 169-78, New Delhi: Rupa.

Verma, Vijay, 1982, *Folk Music of Rajasthan*, Jaipur: Dept. of Tourism, Govt. of Rajasthan.

———, 1988, *The Living Music of Rajasthan*, Delhi: Controller of Publications.